[redacted]

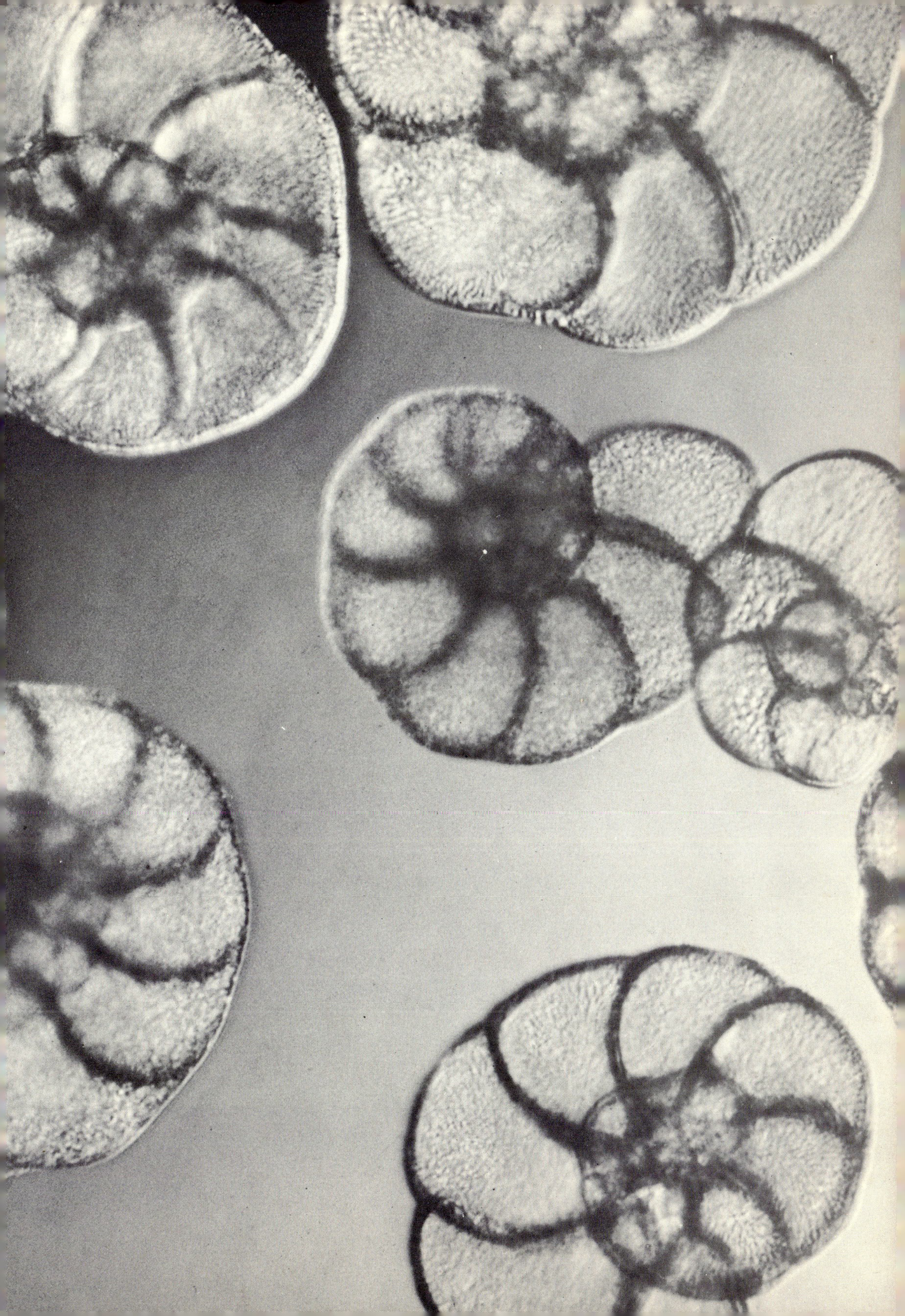

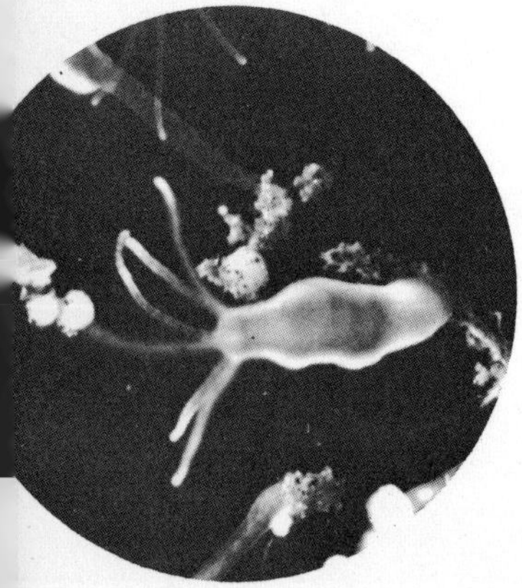
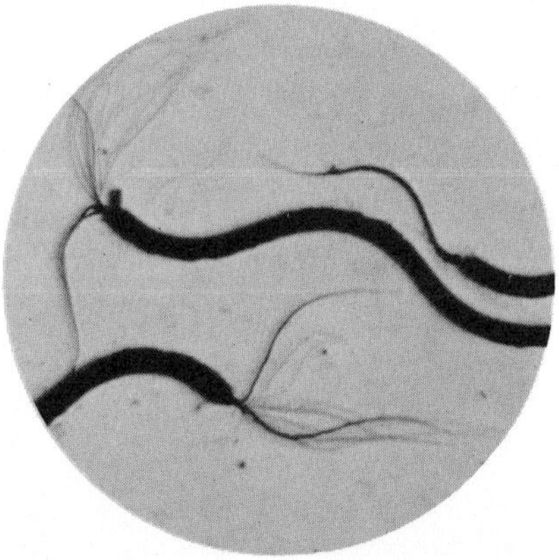
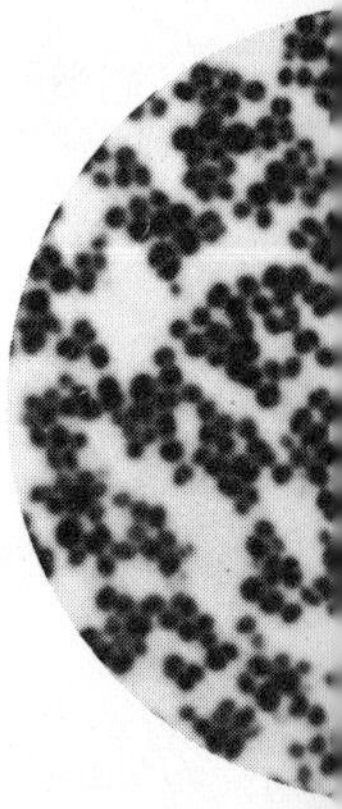

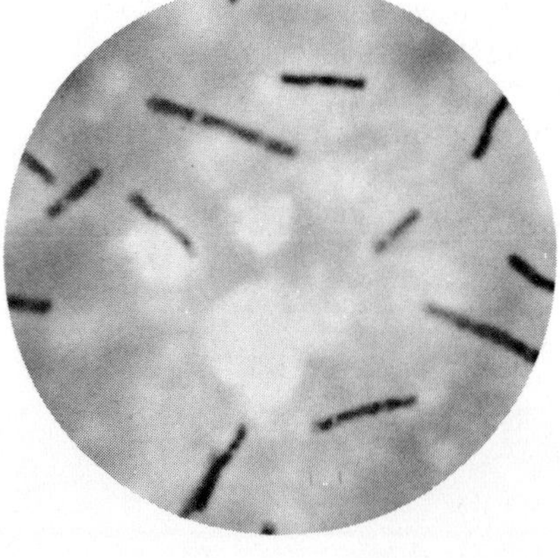

What is life? How did it begin on earth? Does life exist elsewhere in the universe? These are some of the most exciting questions in science today.

In this book Bernard Glemser raises these questions, and tells of the progress that biologists have recently made toward answering them. He also describes some of the great biological discoveries of the past. Finally, he discusses the relationship of simple forms of life to the most complex creature of all—man.

Here is an introduction to biology, the science of life itself.

# All About Biology

# All About Biology

by Bernard Glemser

illustrated with drawings by Eva Cellini

and with photographs

Random House New York

allabout books

For helpful suggestions about this book, the author and the publisher are grateful to Dr. Julius Schwartz, Consultant in Science, Bureau of Curriculum Research, New York City Schools, and to Dr. Selma Silagi, Research Associate, Rockefeller Institute.

The drawings on page 50 accompanied Leeuwenhoek's letter of September 17, 1683, from Delft. The drawings on pages 85, 93, 98, and 106 are adapted, by permission of Dr. Ralph Buchsbaum and The University of Chicago Press, from *Animals Without Backbones* by Ralph Buchsbaum (copyright 1938 and 1948 by The University of Chicago). The drawing on page 126 is adapted, by permission of the Biological Sciences Curriculum Study, from *Biological Science: Molecules to Man* (Houghton Mifflin, 1963).

*Photograph credits: American Museum of Natural History, page 81; American Optical Company, 58 top; Bettmann Archive, 49, 65 bottom; Jack Dermid (from National Audubon Society), 8; Fisher Scientific Company, 58 bottom; Ewing Galloway, 133; Lola Beall Graham (from National Audubon Society), 4; Robert Hermes (from National Audubon Society), 72; A. L. Houwink, Laboratory of Microbiology, Delft, The Netherlands, 53; Mount Wilson and Palomar Observatories, 24; National Institutes of Health, 68; Delbert Philpott, 82; Carl Strüwe (from Monkmeyer), 31 top, 38, 89, 121, 126 bottom; United Press International, 11 bottom; J. G. van Cittert-Eymers, University Museum, Utrecht, The Netherlands, 50 left; Douglas P. Wilson, 31 bottom.*

*Cover: American Museum of Natural History. Endpapers: General Biological Supply House. Frontispiece (ringed anemone): Robert Hermes (from National Audubon Society).*

 Published in New York by Random House, Inc., and simultaneously in Toronto, Canada, by Random House of Canada, Limited.

Library of Congress Catalog Card Number: 63-7802

Designed by Jane Byers

Manufactured in the United States of America

4 466

[redacted]

For my friend
Dr. Ann M. Shearman

# Contents

# All About Biology

# PART ONE

## The Beginnings of Life

*Life began on earth more than two billion years ago. Exactly how it began nobody can say. But, recently, scientists have developed exciting new theories to explain the origin of life and how the two great kingdoms of living things, plants and animals, may have come into existence. These theories may even provide an answer to the question that fascinates mankind: Does life exist elsewhere in the universe?*

# What Is Life?

The great wonder of our world is that it is filled with life.

Wherever you live, you are surrounded by living things. In a city, there are not only multitudes of people. There are dogs and cats and birds and other animals. Trees and grass and flowers of many different kinds grow in the parks. Almost anywhere you look, you can find tiny insects going about their work, and you can see tiny plants growing even between the cracks in the sidewalks.

The tree is alive; the rock is not.

## The Beginnings of Life

In the fields and woods outside the cities, there are so many different kinds of living creatures that you could not possibly count them. The waters of streams and lakes are filled with myriads of living things.

Life abounds everywhere: in the depths of the oceans, and even in the deserts.

But what is life?

What is it that makes a human being or a fish or a tree *alive*?

Scientists cannot really answer these questions. We know a great deal about the way living things are constructed, but life itself is still a great mystery.

Perhaps we should ask these questions in another way. What is the difference between something which is alive, such as an animal or a plant, and something which isn't alive, such as a rock?

You can probably think of several answers.

For example, living things move. You move even while you are asleep. A tree may not appear to move, but its roots are active, and its leaves turn toward the sun all day long.

A rock, though, cannot move by itself. It moves only if it is pushed or if it falls.

Living things respond to heat and cold, to light

and sound, to pain and danger. On a cold day, birds ruffle their feathers to keep themselves warm. On a hot sunny day, dogs and cats seek the shade. Deer become alert at the slightest noise. A baby will cry if it is pricked by a pin. A fox runs away from hunters.

But a rock cannot act in any of these ways. It merely becomes hotter or colder according to the temperature around it.

Living things grow. An elephant begins its life as a tiny speck of living matter which you could hardly see, and grows into a huge animal weighing several tons. A person grows until he is about twenty years old, and his hair and nails continue to grow long afterward. Some animals, such as lobsters and crabs, can even grow new claws and limbs to replace those that have been damaged or lost.

A rock does not grow in the way living things grow. It can only become bigger if other substances stick to it.

Most important of all, living things can reproduce their own kind. Rocks cannot reproduce themselves. But dogs have puppies. Plants produce seeds from which new plants will sprout. Birds lay eggs in their nests, and soon the young birds are flying

Living things reproduce their own kind.

through the air. Human beings have children. And so each kind of life goes on.

Biology—the science of living things—is filled with wonders, and you will read about some of them in the chapters that follow. First, though, we are going to ask a very important question:

How did life begin?

# How Life Began

Scientists cannot say exactly how life began on earth. They can only develop theories to explain what may have happened.

Here is the story of one of the most interesting of these theories.

## Stanley Miller's Experiment

Not long ago, in 1952, a young American scientist named Stanley L. Miller carried out an experiment that made him famous. He was only 23 years old.

The experiment was quite simple.

He used glass tubing, a flask in which water could be boiled continuously, and a device for making a strong electric spark.

Then he arranged for certain gases to circulate through the glass tubing in such a way that the gases passed over the electric spark.

He used these gases:

Hydrogen, which is the lightest of all gases and, in fact, the lightest of all chemical substances. There are enormous quantities of it throughout the universe.

Ammonia, a poisonous gas composed of hydrogen and nitrogen.

Methane, another poisonous gas, composed of hydrogen and carbon. It is found in marshes and mines where vegetation is decaying.

For a week these gases passed through the glass tubing over the electric spark, and bubbled through the boiling water.

Nothing very special seemed to happen. After the first day the water in the flask had turned pink. By the end of the week the water was a deep cloudy red.

Below: Stanley Miller. Right: a simplified diagram of the apparatus he built to duplicate the conditions under which life probably began.

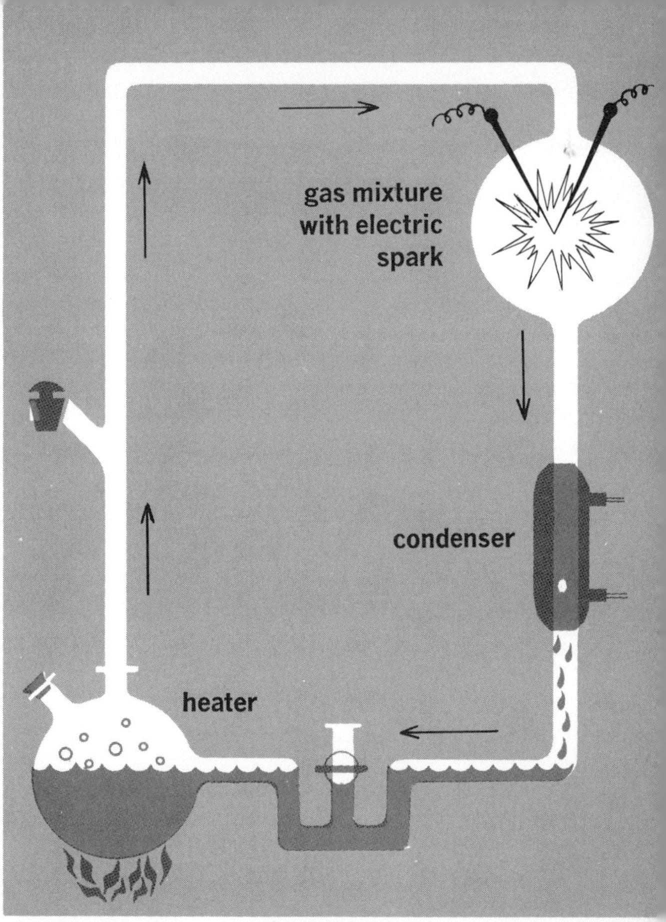

Then, with great care, Miller analyzed the water in the flask.

And now came the discovery that brought him world-wide fame. For the water contained several chemicals called AMINO ACIDS which had not been there at the beginning of the experiment.

Why should this cause such a stir?

Because amino acids are the building blocks of substances called PROTEINS. And proteins are the most important part of all living things. The word protein, indeed, means "of first importance." About half of the solid matter in your body is composed of thousands of different kinds of proteins. All of these proteins are built up from different combinations of amino acids.

This is why Dr. Miller's experiment caused so much excitement. He had found a way to make some of the building blocks of living matter!

But there was still another reason why the experiment was so remarkable. To explain this we have to go back to the very beginning of the earth.

## In the Beginning

According to some calculations, our earth began its

existence about five billion years ago.

Nothing could possibly live on the earth then. Its surface was too hot.

Also, its atmosphere was poisonous, consisting of ammonia, methane, hydrogen, and water vapor. In addition, ultraviolet rays poured down from the blazing sun—the dangerous rays that cause sunburn. These alone, probably, would have destroyed any living thing.

Then, as the earth's surface cooled, the water vapor in the atmosphere condensed and turned into rain. The sky was torn by violent electric storms. Lightning flashed continuously, from cloud to cloud and from the sky to the ground. Scientists believe that this tremendous rainstorm went on for millions and millions of years. So much rain fell that the oceans of the earth were formed.

How could life have begun under such fearsome conditions?

Let us look at Stanley Miller's experiment again.

What he really constructed was a sort of tiny model of our earth as it was at the beginning, billions of years ago.

The gases passing through the glass tubing represented the earth's atmosphere.

Life began in the oceans, scientists believe, under violent conditions.

The strong electric spark represented the violent electric storms, and also the fierce ultraviolet rays that poured down on the earth from the sun.

The water in the flask represented the oceans.

Stanley Miller's experiment lasted only one week. In that week, several amino acids were created.

In the same way, many scientists believe, amino acids were created during those millions and millions of years when the earth's atmosphere was so hot and stormy.

And those amino acids were the first building blocks of life.

## The Cooling Earth

The earth continued to cool for more than a billion years. During this period a new atmosphere formed. It consisted of water vapor; a gas, nitrogen; and another gas, carbon dioxide, which is composed of carbon and oxygen.

Streams and rivers flowed over the lands which had not been submerged by the great rainstorms, washing vast quantities of chemicals out of the rocks and carrying them into the steaming oceans.

Volcanoes erupted constantly, throwing up white-hot lava from the inside of the earth. Chemical substances from this lava, too, were washed into the oceans.

As a result, the oceans were so filled with chemicals of many kinds that they were like great bowls of hot soup. More and more particles of amino acids were produced by the action of lightning and the powerful ultraviolet rays of the sun.

## Combinations of Amino Acids

It is not difficult to understand what may have happened in the next stage.

There are about twenty kinds of amino acids—nearly as many as the letters in our alphabet.

Let us imagine, then, that all the oceans of the earth were filled with billions and billions of tiny scraps of paper, each scrap with a letter of the alphabet on it.

Now imagine these scraps of paper being tossed by waves and currents, day and night, year after year.

Some of the scraps, sooner or later, would stick to each other. They might form a word like NKPI, which isn't really a word; or KIPN, which still isn't really a word; or PINK, which is a word you recognize at once.

Other scraps might form EBUL, or UELB, or—another word you will recognize—BLUE.

Then, perhaps after many years, two sets of letters might stick together, forming PINK-PINK or BLUE-BLUE or perhaps PINK-BLUE.

Many of these combinations would have no meaning. But if you waited long enough—millions of years—you would get more and more interesting combinations of letters.

This is how life may have begun in the oceans. There were still no forms of life that you could recognize, even with a microscope. There were merely amino acids, joining together in different combinations.

But when amino acids join together in certain special combinations, proteins are produced. And it is chiefly from proteins that living matter is constructed.

# Proteins: Molecules of Life

Let us imagine that an astronaut from a distant planet in outer space visited our earth about two billion years ago, searching for signs of life.

If he had brought no special equipment, he would be disappointed.

On land, he would find nothing but stark, barren rocks. There would be no trace of plants or animals. There would be no trace of intelligent beings like himself.

He would find nothing alive in the oceans. There would be only particles of various chemical substances, far too small to be seen by the naked eye.

And there would be no food of any kind for him to eat.

He would probably send a radio message back to his home planet: "Absolutely no signs of life here. Atmosphere poisonous. Temperature too hot for comfort. Am leaving at once."

But let us imagine, instead, that the space traveler was a highly trained scientist, and that his space ship was equipped with every kind of scientific instrument, including a powerful electron microscope.

The land would still appear to be barren.

But when he analyzed the chemical substances in the sea, he would find that some of the particles were very complicated. With the help of his instruments he would discover that these particles consisted of long chains of amino acids, joined together to form many different shapes. Some might be long slender fibers, some might be coiled up like a ball.

When he made this discovery, he would probably send a radio message to his home planet: "Have identified various proteins. Life may be beginning on this planet. Am staying to investigate further."

## Giant Molecules

You can get some idea of how complicated proteins are by comparing them to another substance that is vital to life: water.

The smallest particle of any chemical substance is called a MOLECULE. A molecule of water, for example, is made up of two atoms of hydrogen and one atom of oxygen.

But a molecule of a protein found in milk, lactoglobulin, is made up of:

*1,864 atoms of carbon*
*3,012 atoms of hydrogen*
*576 atoms of oxygen*
*468 atoms of nitrogen*
*21 atoms of sulfur*

Still another way of comparing substances is by their molecular weight—which means the weight of all the atoms in one molecule of the substance.

Hydrogen has a molecular weight of 1.

But the smallest protein has a molecular weight of about 13,000. Some of the larger proteins have molecular weights ranging up to 10,000,000.

So it is no wonder that scientists often refer to

these protein molecules as giant molecules, even though you would need a very powerful microscope to see them.

## Bubbles of Life

None of these giant protein molecules could have existed two billion years ago, when our imaginary astronaut from outer space was searching our earth for signs of life. Lactoglobulin, for example, is found in milk; but animals which make milk were not yet in existence.

So the proteins our astronaut found would have been fairly simple ones.

But if he arrived at the right time in our earth's history, he would have found some tiny specks floating in the warm soupy oceans that would have filled him with the greatest excitement.

Through his microscope he would see that they were like tiny transparent bubbles containing a watery, colorless jelly. This jelly consisted of molecules of many different sorts of proteins, together with molecules of other chemicals.

You could be sure that our astronaut would report this discovery at once. For the colorless jelly was a substance we call PROTOPLASM, which means "basic material of life."

And those tiny transparent bubbles floating in the early oceans may have been the first forms of life to appear on our earth.

## Life in the Universe

This theory about the beginning of life has led to new ideas about life on other worlds.

Many of us have wondered as we gaze up at the sky on a starry night: Are there living beings up there like ourselves, looking across space at us as we look at them?

As far as the planets of our own solar system are concerned, the answer is: No.

Mercury is too close to the sun, and therefore it is too hot to support life as we know it. Venus, also, is probably too hot.

Mars is an exciting possibility, because some kind of vegetation seems to exist on it. In the near future, space probes may tell us more about Mars.

The outermost planets, Jupiter, Saturn, Uranus, Neptune, and Pluto, are so far from the sun—and therefore so cold—that there is little possibility of life existing on them.

So, of the nine planets in our solar system, only one (to the best of our knowledge) has living beings on it: the planet we inhabit, the earth.

Our sun, though, is only one star in a great galaxy of stars called the Milky Way.

Altogether, the Milky Way contains between 50 billion and 200 billion stars.

A vast number of these stars came into existence at about the same time and in the same way as our sun.

Many of them probably have planets of their own, formed of the same kind of materials as our planet. Probably, too, many of these planets have gone through the same stages of development as the earth.

If this is so, then life in some form may have developed on them, just as life has developed here.

But the Milky Way is only one of an enormous number of galaxies in the universe. Astronomers can see more than a billion galaxies with their present telescopes.

Scientists have calculated that, if life has developed on only one planet in a million, then life might exist on a million billion (1,000,000,000,000,000) planets scattered through the universe.

## Proteins: Molecules of Life

And on many of these planets, life may have started in the same way that scientists think it started here.

First, over millions of years, amino acids were formed.

Then, over more millions of years, these amino acids combined to form many kinds of proteins.

And then, over still more millions of years, these proteins combined to form the marvelous substance of life, protoplasm.

There are countless galaxies in the universe—each, perhaps, the home of life.

# The First Plants and Animals

Those tiny bubbles of living material, the earliest form of life on our planet, could exist only in the oceans.

One reason was this: On land, the burning rays of the sun would probably have destroyed them very quickly.

Another reason was that they needed food in order to stay alive, and grow, and multiply. But there was no food on the land, which still consisted of hot barren rocks. The oceans, though, were filled with nourishing chemical substances.

So the tiny organisms remained in the oceans. They were protected from the sun's heat. They had vast supplies of food. And they were even safe from attack, because there were no other forms of life to menace them.

But this could not go on forever.

As millions of years passed, and as the tiny organisms multiplied, the nourishing substances in the oceans were gradually used up. Eventually, instead of an abundance, there was a shortage of food.

This was a grave problem. Unless a new way of getting food was found, life would come to an end.

## The First Plants

Fortunately, some of the tiny organisms were able to solve the problem by a method so complicated that we are still not sure exactly how it is done.

By using the energy in sunlight, the organisms could make certain kinds of food from water and carbon dioxide.

This amazing process is called PHOTOSYNTHESIS. The term comes from two Greek words, *photo,* "light," and *synthesis,* "putting together."

By means of photosynthesis, the tiny organisms could make food substances called CARBOHYDRATES, which are essential for the energy of living things. Sugars are carbohydrates, and so are starches.

This was not all.

By using the carbohydrates together with various chemicals which could be obtained from the water around them, the tiny organisms could go on to make amino acids.

Then they could go yet a step further, and put the amino acids together to make proteins.

In this way they had carbohydrates for energy, as well as amino acids and proteins that enabled them to grow and multiply.

The organisms which first used photosynthesis to make their food are of tremendous importance to us. They were the forerunners of one of the great kingdoms of life, the plant kingdom.

## The First Animals

But there were also some organisms that found another, and much easier, way of getting their food. They simply ate other living organisms.

By doing this, they did not have to go through

the complicated process of photosynthesis to make carbohydrates. They ate the carbohydrates in plants. They also acquired amino acids from the plants they ate, and formed their own special proteins from them.

These organisms were the forerunners of the other great kingdom of life—the animal kingdom.

Even now, more than a billion years later, plants (with a few exceptions) make their food by photosynthesis, and animals obtain their food by eating other living things. This is one of the most important differences between the two kingdoms of life.

Perhaps the best way to understand how living things developed is to draw the letter Y. The straight upright stem represents the first living organisms. One arm, branching off, represents the beginning of plant life. The other arm represents the beginning of animal life.

This branching off was very gradual. It took millions and millions of years. During this time some organisms came into existence that were neither plants nor animals.

The descendants of these organisms still exist. Some are plants which are like animals. Some are animals which are like plants.

For example, there is a tiny organism named *Euglena.* It moves through the water by means of a long thin filament, like a whip, which acts as a sort of propeller. Scientists call this whip by its Latin name, *flagellum.* Organisms which possess these whip-like filaments are called Flagellates.

Now, when the Euglena is in daylight, it can make its food by photosynthesis. So it seems to be a plant.

But if it is in darkness, it will get food by eating other little organisms. So it seems to be an animal.

To avoid argument, the little Euglena is sometimes referred to as a PLANT-ANIMAL.

Other organisms, which you would scarcely recognize as plants, are the diatoms. Each one lives in a box. There are thousands of different kinds, and they can be found in the oceans, in rivers, and even in ponds. The boxes in which they live are made of a glass-like substance called silica. Generally, each box consists of two lids, decorated with delicate and beautiful patterns.

Tiny as they are, the diatoms are of the greatest importance. Billions and billions of them, together with other tiny plants and animals, float in the oceans and are carried along by the tides and cur-

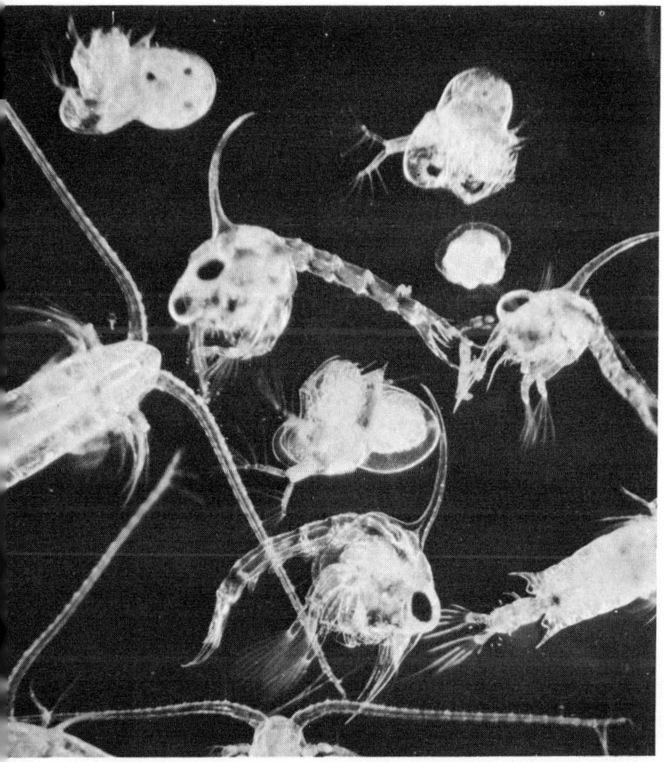

Tiny plants and animals known as plankton are the food for other living things in the ocean. Above: the beautiful "boxes" of the plants called diatoms (magnified 225 times). At left: living animal plankton (magnified 18 times).

rents. Scientists call these little organisms PLANKTON, which comes from a Greek word meaning "wanderers."

Small fish live by eating plankton, and bigger fish live by eating the small fish. So, directly or indirectly, nearly every animal that lives in water depends on plankton.

## The Importance of the First Plants

As we look back now, we can see that the first plants changed the entire history of the earth. They made it possible for all future life to develop.

They not only changed the face of the earth. They even changed the atmosphere surrounding the earth.

At first, as we have seen, the earth's atmosphere consisted of a mixture of gases: hydrogen, ammonia, methane, and water vapor.

Later, after the great rains, a new atmosphere came into being. This consisted of water vapor, nitrogen, and carbon dioxide.

Living things still could not emerge from the oceans onto the land. Even if they could have breathed this atmosphere they would probably have been destroyed by the burning rays of the sun.

Carbon dioxide, though, is soluble in water.

Some of the carbon dioxide in the atmosphere became dissolved in the oceans.

The first plants used this dissolved carbon dioxide to make their food by photosynthesis. At the same time, they released oxygen.

Very, very gradually the carbon dioxide in the atmosphere was consumed by the plants and replaced by oxygen. Once again a new atmosphere came into being, the third in the history of the earth. Nearly four-fifths of this atmosphere was nitrogen; nearly one-fifth was oxygen. Only a small fraction was carbon dioxide, but this was enough for the needs of the plants.

Then another remarkable change took place.

High in the atmosphere, some of the oxygen turned into a special form of oxygen called ozone. The ozone acted like an invisible screen around the earth, preventing most of the fierce ultraviolet rays of the sun from reaching the earth's surface.

And, at last, perhaps 350 million years ago, living things could safely come out of the oceans onto land. Primitive plants and tiny primitive animals crept out onto the shores and began the task of making the earth green and fertile.

Life could not come ashore from the ocean until the ozone layer developed, providing protection from the sun's harmful rays.

So life on earth was made possible by those first plants which developed the marvelous process of photosynthesis.

Plants still supply the precious oxygen we breathe: every year they provide us with 400 billion tons of oxygen. Nine-tenths of this amount comes from the plant life that inhabits the oceans. All the grass and all the trees and all the other vegetation on all the continents of the earth provide only one-tenth of the oxygen in the air.

# PART TWO

# Some Great Discoveries in Biology

*Most of our knowledge of the science of life has come to us only in the last 350 years. During this time, thousands and thousands of scientists worked to discover the facts on which our present knowledge is based.*

*You will meet some of them in the next three chapters: a scientist in Flanders puzzling over a willow tree; a Dutchman looking at drops of water through a new invention called a microscope; an Englishman wondering about "bladders of air" in a slice of cork; an Italian experimenting with various pieces of meat; a brilliant Frenchman whose ideas were to save millions of lives.*

*These were among the great pathfinders in biology. Their names and their work will never be forgotten.*

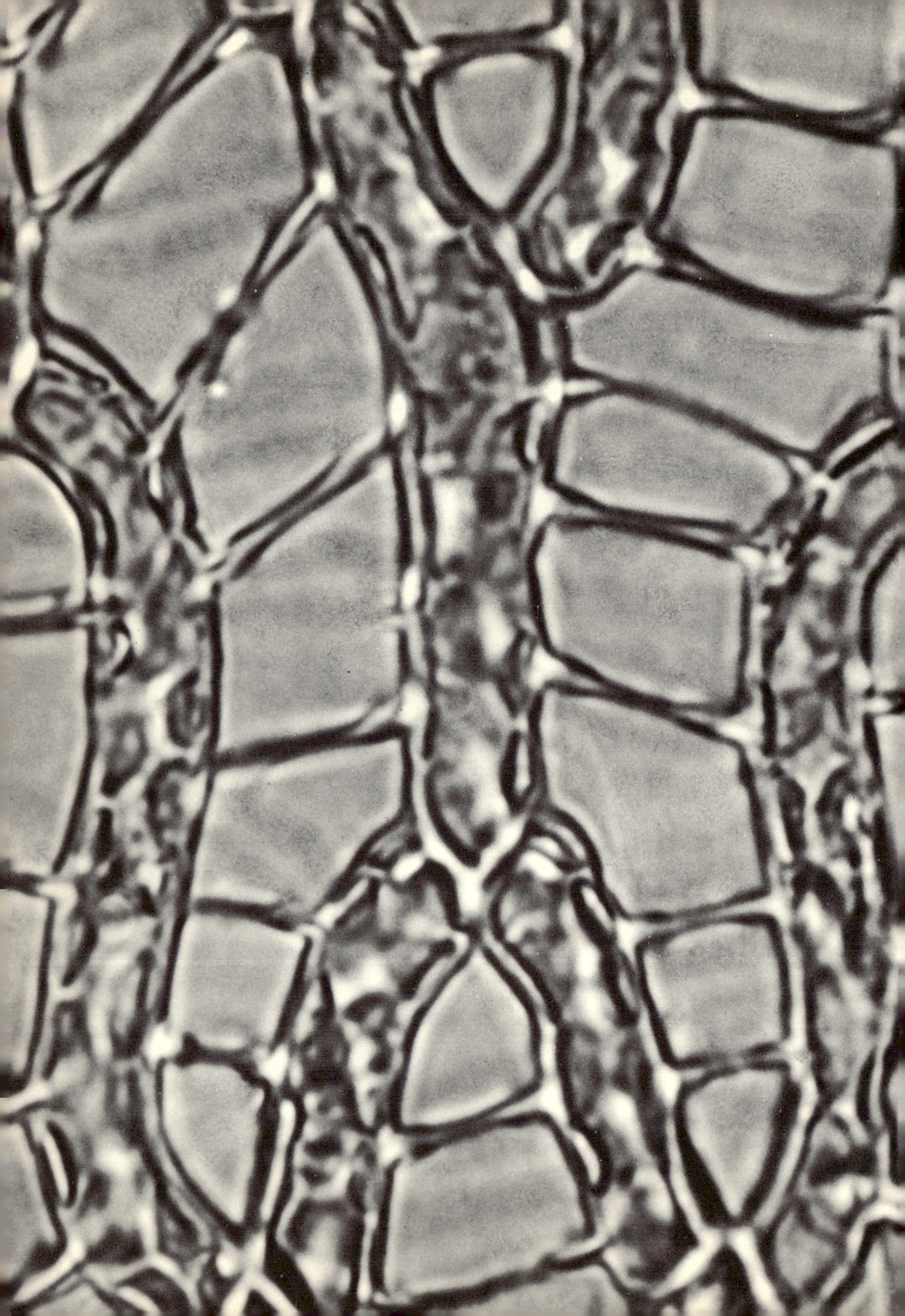

# The Scientist and the Willow Tree

Sometimes a scientist carefully performs an experiment, expecting a certain result, and then gets a quite different result.

This is what happened to a Flemish scientist named Jan Baptista van Helmont, who lived from 1577 to 1644. When you read about him you should bear in mind that very little was known then about the science of life. Many of the simplest facts of biology still had to be discovered.

Living cells in a leaf (magnified 1800 times).

# Helmont's Experiment

In those days most people believed that plants obtained their nourishment from the soil. It was accepted as a fact that the blacker and "richer" the earth, the better would plants grow. Some people still believe this.

About the year 1625, Helmont decided to carry out an experiment to learn exactly how much nourishment the soil supplied to a growing plant.

First, he dried two hundred pounds of soil in a furnace. He put the dry soil into a large pot.

He moistened the soil with rain water, and planted in it a small willow tree, weighing five pounds.

He put a cover over the pot to prevent dust from getting into it; and he did little more except to water the soil regularly with rain water.

Then, after five years, he removed the willow tree from the pot and weighed it.

The willow tree had grown considerably. It had gained 164 pounds.

Next, he weighed the soil in the pot to find out how much of it had been used up to nourish the growing willow tree. He reasoned that if the soil

Helmont's willow tree, before and after his important experiment.

supplied the tree's nourishment, it should have lost about 164 pounds.

But to his astonishment he discovered that the soil weighed almost exactly the same as when he started his experiment, five years earlier. It had lost only about two ounces.

This was very strange. Where had all the weight of the willow tree come from, if not from the rich black earth in the pot?

After a great deal of thought, Helmont finally decided that the weight must have come from the water which he had added to the soil so regularly. This appeared to be the only answer, because there seemed to be no other source from which the weight could have come.

He was partly right. The tree did get some of its weight from the rain water. It also took very small quantities of minerals from the soil.

But Helmont didn't realize that there was another source of nourishment, apart from the water and the soil. True, it was invisible. Yet he was surrounded by it, and so was his willow tree.

That source was the air.

## Nourishment From the Air

Few people think of air as a source of food. But air contains carbon dioxide, which consists, as we have seen, of carbon and oxygen. It is this carbon which is the basis of the food of all plants. Each year, all thc plants in the world extract from the air about 150 billion tons of carbon for use in their food.

This is part of the explanation of how Helmont's

little willow tree gained its weight. The full explanation did not come until about two hundred years after Helmont carried out his experiment. It took scientists all this time to learn that plants make carbohydrates from carbon dioxide (which comes from the air) and water (which, mostly, the plants take in through their roots).

The way plants make carbohydrates, as we saw in the previous chapter, is by photosynthesis.

When scientists learn all the secrets of photosynthesis, human beings may no longer have to eat plants. It might be possible to build great factories to manufacture the carbohydrates, and perhaps even the proteins, that we need for our food. People living in some of the poorer countries in the world would never have any fears of famine if their food could be made directly from water plus carbon dioxide from the air.

First, though, scientists must learn more about a marvelous substance called CHLOROPHYLL.

Chlorophyll is the green substance in leaves. Its name comes from *chloro,* "green," and *phyll,* "leaf." It is the chlorophyll that enables photosynthesis to take place.

Somehow chlorophyll can trap sunlight, and use

the energy in the sunlight to make carbohydrates.

Here is a simplified explanation of what happens during photosynthesis. To make it easier to understand, we will discuss it in two stages.

*In the first stage,* the chlorophyll in the leaf absorbs sunlight.

Within the leaf there is a small amount of water.

The chlorophyll now uses the energy of the sunlight to split the water in the leaf into hydrogen and oxygen.

Most of the oxygen is released into the air.

Most of the hydrogen remains in the leaf.

*In the second stage,* the chlorophyll uses the energy of the sunlight to combine the hydrogen (which it obtained from splitting water) with carbon dioxide (which the leaf has obtained from the air).

Then, after several complicated changes, the hydrogen and the carbon dioxide are finally combined in such a way that a carbohydrate is produced.

This carbohydrate is a sugar called glucose.

Later, using glucose as its most important building block, the plant can make the amino acids and proteins that it needs.

Something else happens during photosynthesis that is of the greatest importance to us. A constant supply of oxygen is released into the air by the plants. We need this oxygen. At the same time, carbon dioxide, which would poison us if we breathed too much of it, is used up.

All this is possible because of that marvelous green substance, chlorophyll.

## Why Animals Depend on Plants

But there is still more to the story of plants and photosynthesis.

No animal (except the tiny plant-animals such as the Euglena) possesses chlorophyll. There are greenish animals, such as some lizards and grasshoppers, but this green is only protective coloration that enables the animals to hide from their enemies.

Since animals do not possess chlorophyll, they cannot carry out photosynthesis to make the carbohydrates which they must have for energy.

Furthermore, since they cannot make carbohydrates, they cannot make amino acids. And, without amino acids, they cannot make proteins.

Therefore, animals can do only one thing to obtain carbohydrates, amino acids, and proteins: They must eat green plants in some form.

Big fish, as we have seen, eat little fish, which feed on tiny plants. So, in a way, the big fish are eating plants which have already been converted into carbohydrates, amino acids, and proteins.

Cattle eat only green plants, from which they make all the substances in their big heavy bodies.

Lions eat cattle. So, in a way, the lions are eating green plants that have already been converted into carbohydrates, amino acids, and proteins.

This is equally true of human beings, who eat meat and fish and drink milk, in addition to eating fruit and vegetables.

So, all animals—those that live on land as well as those that live in water—owe their lives to plants. Without plants we could not exist.

# What the Microscopes Revealed

In 1665, only forty years after Helmont experimented with the willow tree, an English scientist named Robert Hooke published a description of some thin slices of cork which he had been studying under a microscope.

Microscopes had been invented only fifty or sixty years earlier. There were not many of them yet, and these were very crude compared with later microscopes. Nobody realized that they would save more lives than any other instrument that man has devised.

## Hooke's Discovery

Hooke was interested in many aspects of science. He constructed telescopes to study the planets. He invented the spiral spring that is used in watches. And he even built a machine to solve problems in arithmetic. But he is remembered now principally for his study of cork.

Cork comes from the outside of a tree called the cork oak. It is very light and tough. Since the earliest times it has been used to make stoppers for casks and bottles, as well as floats for fishermen's nets.

When Hooke examined a thin slice of cork under his microscope he was surprised to find that it was constructed in a strange way. It was composed, in his own words, of a great many "small Boxes or Bladders of Air."

He called each small box a CELL. He took the word from the Latin *cella,* meaning "chamber" or "room."

He was even more surprised when he estimated

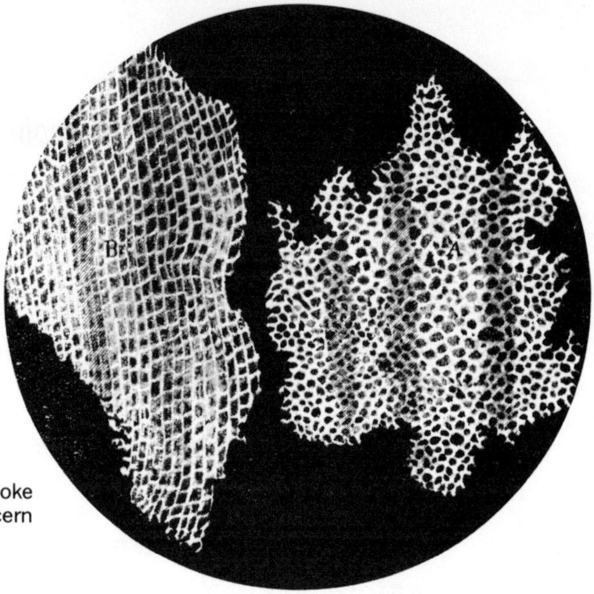

Cells in a thin slice of cork, as seen by Robert Hooke in 1665. The study of the cell remains the concern of many biologists today.

the number of these little boxes. According to his calculations, there were more than a billion in a cubic inch of cork.

Hooke went on to study various vegetables and plants, such as carrots and ferns; and he found that these, also, were built of "small Boxes." Even the shaft of a feather was built in the same way.

It was a great discovery. We still use the word that Robert Hooke used, cells, although we no longer think of cells as "small Boxes or Bladders of Air."

## Leeuwenhoek's Discovery

Only twelve years later, Hooke was involved in another great discovery.

In the town of Delft, in Holland, there lived a man named Antony van Leeuwenhoek, whose hobby was grinding lenses which he made into microscopes. Because of the great care with which he made them, his microscopes were better than any that had been made so far. They could magnify objects as much as two hundred times.

A number of scientists in London had formed an organization called the Royal Society. When they heard about Leeuwenhoek's wonderful microscopes, they invited him to write to the Royal Society, so that they could be kept informed of anything new

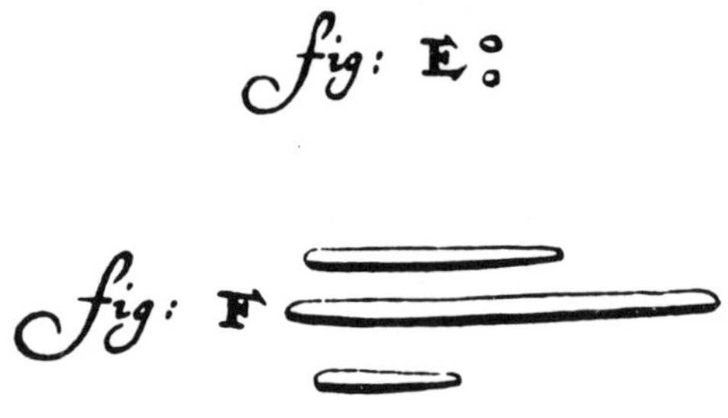


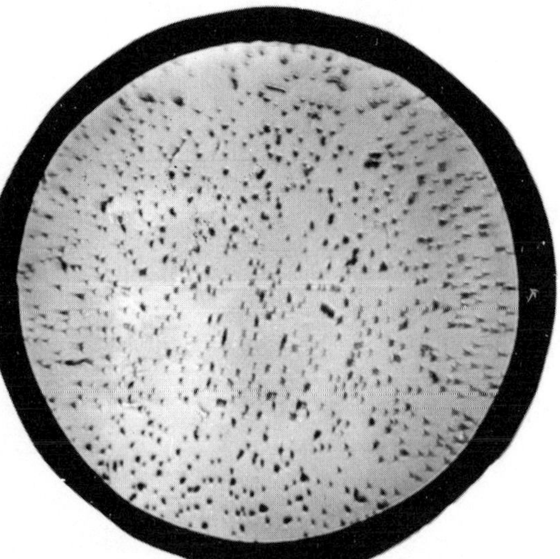

Top: Two of Leeuwenhoek's drawings of what he saw in a drop of water. Left: A photograph taken recently through one of Leeuwenhoek's microscopes. If you look closely, you can see what he saw—many round bacteria and a few longer rodlike ones.

that his microscopes revealed.

He wrote them many letters. Then, in 1676, he wrote them a letter which was so extraordinary that the scientists of the Royal Society could hardly believe it was true.

He had already described to them how he had seen animalcules in stagnant water. (By "animalcules" he meant strange, animal-like creatures, so tiny that they could be seen only through a microscope.) Now he described what he had seen in some "pepper water" —that is, water in which a few grains of pepper had been dissolved, and which had stood untouched for about three weeks.

There were not only animalcules like those he had seen earlier. There were many new kinds of animalcules, swimming around in thousands. In addition, there were curious things that looked like little sticks, or rods, very much smaller than the smallest animalcules.

This was so strange that the Royal Society asked other scientists to check Leeuwenhoek's discovery. One of these scientists was Robert Hooke.

The task took over a year, because first a microscope had to be built that was as good as the microscope used by Leeuwenhoek.

At last, Hooke prepared some pepper water and examined it under the new microscope; and he found that Leeuwenhoek was perfectly right. He reported to the Royal Society that there were, indeed, "an infinite number of animalls" in the pepper water. But, Hooke went on, "These were gygantick monsters in comparison to a lesser sort which almost filled the water."

By "lesser sort" he meant the little sticks, or rods, which Leeuwenhoek had seen.

Hooke would have been surprised to know that the creatures he described as "gygantick monsters" were actually tiny animals each composed of a single cell. We now call them PROTOZOA, which means "first animals." More than 15,000 different species of Protozoa have been discovered since they were first seen by Leeuwenhoek and Hooke.

The tiny rods in the pepper water were also living organisms. Each of these, also, was composed of a single cell, much smaller than the one-celled Protozoa. Scientists have called them by several different names in the past three centuries. First they were called GERMS. Then they were called MICROBES. But now we usually call them BACTERIA, which comes from a Greek word meaning "rod" or "staff," although not all bacteria have this shape. Traces of them have been found in rocks that are a billion years old.

If you could examine a collection of bacteria under a very powerful microscope, you might think you were seeing creatures of science fiction. There would be small bacteria and big bacteria. There would be some with one whiplike filament, or flagellum, some with tufts of flagella, some with flagella all around them.

But after you studied them carefully, you would

A bacterium with tufts of flagella (magnified 45,000 times).

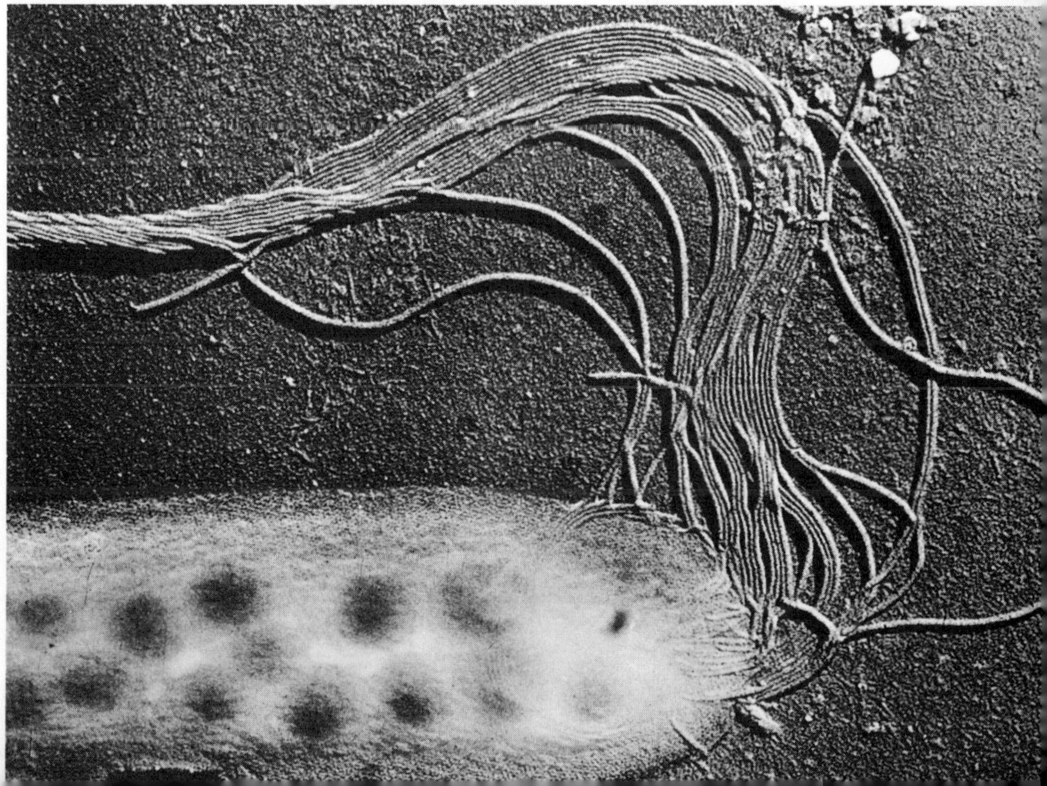

find that they could be arranged into three kinds.

Some are shaped like rods. These are called BACILLI, which has the same meaning as the word bacteria—little rods or sticks. (The singular is *bacillus.*)

Others are like little corkscrews. These are called SPIRILLA, which means "spiral-shaped." (The singular is *spirillum.*)

Still others are like small beads, and these are called COCCI, which means "berries." (The singular is *coccus.*) Often the cocci join together in a chain, or clump into a little ball.

You know, of course, that many illnesses are caused by bacteria. Fortunately, scientists have discovered powerful new drugs which will kill most of the bacteria that are harmful to us.

## Help From Bacteria

It would be wrong, though, to think of all bacteria as our enemies. Vast numbers of bacteria exist in the world; and only a few, relatively, cause disease. A scientist once calculated that only one of every 30,000 bacteria in the United States is harmful to any plant, animal, or human being.

Many kinds of bacteria are, in fact, of the greatest

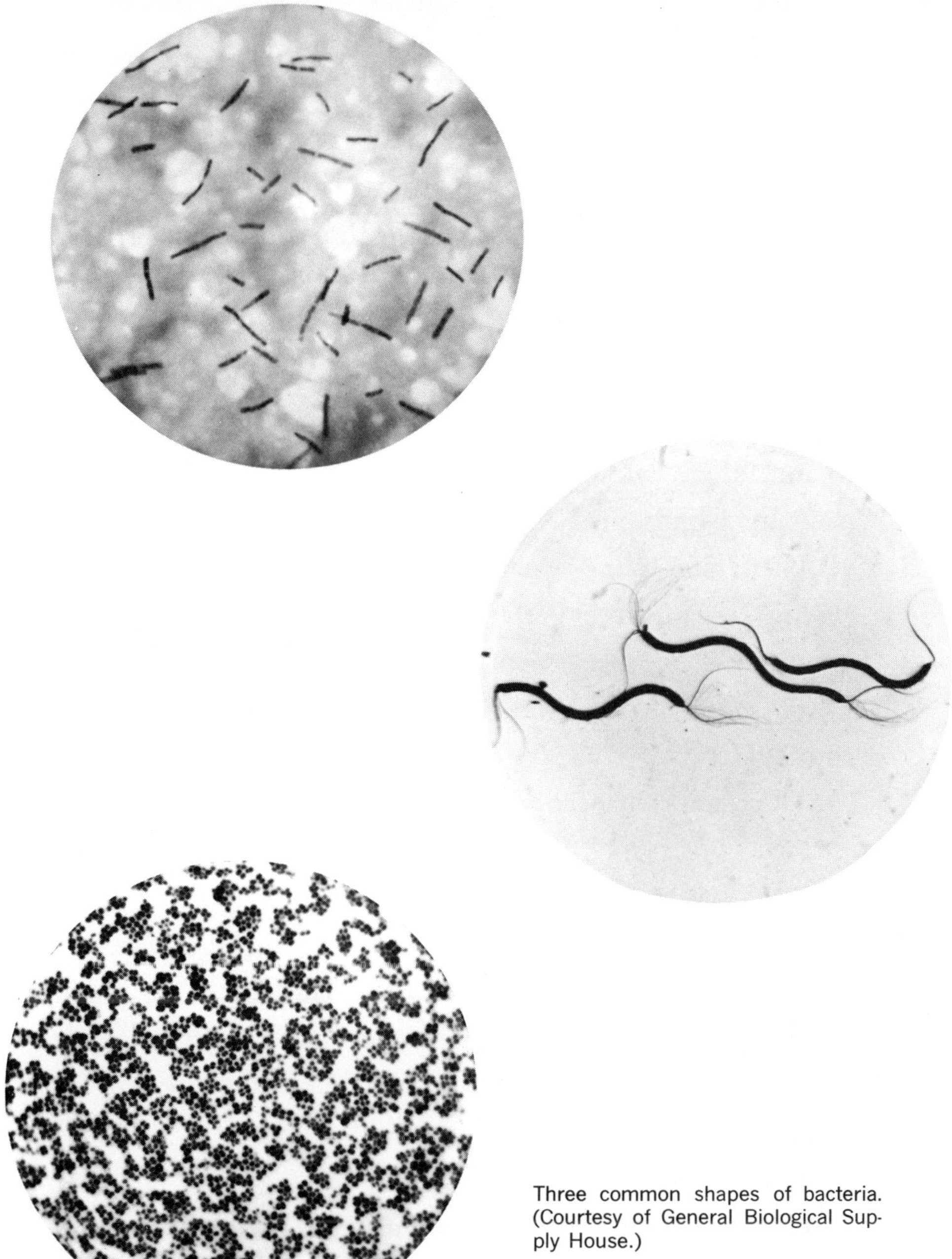

Three common shapes of bacteria. (Courtesy of General Biological Supply House.)

benefit to us.

For example, certain bacteria in the soil provide plants with nitrogen, which is essential for making amino acids and proteins.

So, without these special bacteria, there might be no plants growing on land; and, of course, without plants there would be no animals on land and no human beings.

There are many ways in which bacteria serve other living organisms. Perhaps the most important way, strange as it may seem, is by living inside animals.

To explain this, we have to look at plants a little more closely.

All plants are composed of cells. There are tiny plants consisting of a single cell, but larger plants consist of multitudes of cells. A blade of grass is made up of millions of cells.

The same is true of animals. There are tiny animals which consist of one cell, but larger animals consist of a great many cells. A human being is made up of at least 10 trillion (10,000,000,000,000) cells.

However, the cells of a plant are different from the cells of an animal in a very special way.

Around the outside of the cells of a plant there

is a wall of a tough substance called cellulose. The cells of an animal do not have this cellulose wall.

Cellulose is a carbohydrate, and it is a very important substance. Wood is largely cellulose, and so is cotton. We make an enormous variety of things from cellulose, including paper, cellophane, rayon, and even dynamite.

You might think that plants have a wall of cellulose around their cells to protect them from being eaten. For, although the inside of the cell can be digested quite easily, the outside—consisting of tough cellulose—is normally indigestible.

As a result, the precious materials inside the plant cell are imprisoned within the cellulose wall.

There is an easy way in which the cellulose wall can be broken down, and that is by cooking the plant. Human beings can use this method, but animals cannot.

Fortunately, there are other ways in which the cellulose wall can be digested.

Some insects are able to digest cellulose by means of substances called CELLULASES.

But animals like cows and horses, which feed entirely on plants, do not have cellulases. Instead, their digestive tracts contain great numbers of certain kinds

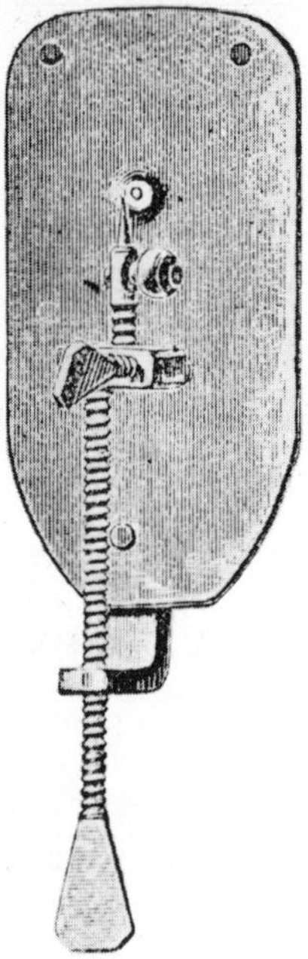

With his ingenious homemade apparatus (left), Leeuwenhoek could magnify objects up to 200 times. Today's electron microscopes (bottom) magnify up to 250,000 times.

of bacteria. These bacteria do the highly important work of digesting the cellulose wall, and so the substances within the plant cells can be released.

Another important role that bacteria play is making vitamins for us inside our bodies. One of these is vitamin K, which helps the blood to clot. Clotting stops the bleeding when we cut ourselves. Bacteria also make many of the B-complex vitamins.

Recently, scientists did some important research on this subject.

Their problem was that in parts of Australia many sheep were dying of starvation. Yet the animals grazed on rich pastures and seemed to have plenty to eat.

Eventually, the scientists discovered that the sheep were dying because of a lack of a metal called cobalt in the soil. By scattering only one ounce of cobalt on the pastures, 800 sheep could be kept perfectly healthy for a whole year.

The most surprising thing about this discovery was that it was not the sheep themselves that needed the cobalt.

Certain bacteria inside the sheep required tiny amounts of cobalt in order to manufacture a special vitamin, $B_{12}$. Without this vitamin the sheep became sick and died.

But when cobalt was scattered on the soil, plants absorbed small amounts of the cobalt. The sheep ate the plants containing the cobalt. Then the bacteria inside the sheep could use the cobalt to make the vitamin $B_{12}$. So the sheep were strong and healthy.

# Germs from Germs, Cells from Cells

The discovery of cells and the discovery of bacteria were tremendous steps forward in man's understanding of life. But, like most great discoveries, they raised many new questions, which were to puzzle scientists for years to come.

For example, when Leeuwenhoek examined the pepper water which had stood for three weeks, he found it teeming with tiny organisms. Where had these organisms come from?

The only answer he could give was that they had

come from the pepper water itself.

Many scientists at this time believed that life could come into existence in this way. It was believed that the soil, by itself, produced earthworms; that the mud in ponds, by itself, produced frogs and snails; that a few grains of corn, left for two or three weeks, would produce mice.

This is known as the theory of SPONTANEOUS GENERATION, which means life coming into existence by itself from nonliving matter.

In 1668, an Italian doctor named Francesco Redi performed an experiment to test this theory.

## Redi's Discovery

If meat is left in the air for several days it often will begin to rot, and small wormlike animals called maggots will crawl out of it.

Maggots look unpleasant, but they are living creatures, and therefore to any biologist they are full of interest.

Redi's experiment was simple. He put pieces of different kinds of meat in several jars. He covered some of the jars with fine muslin, and left the other jars uncovered.

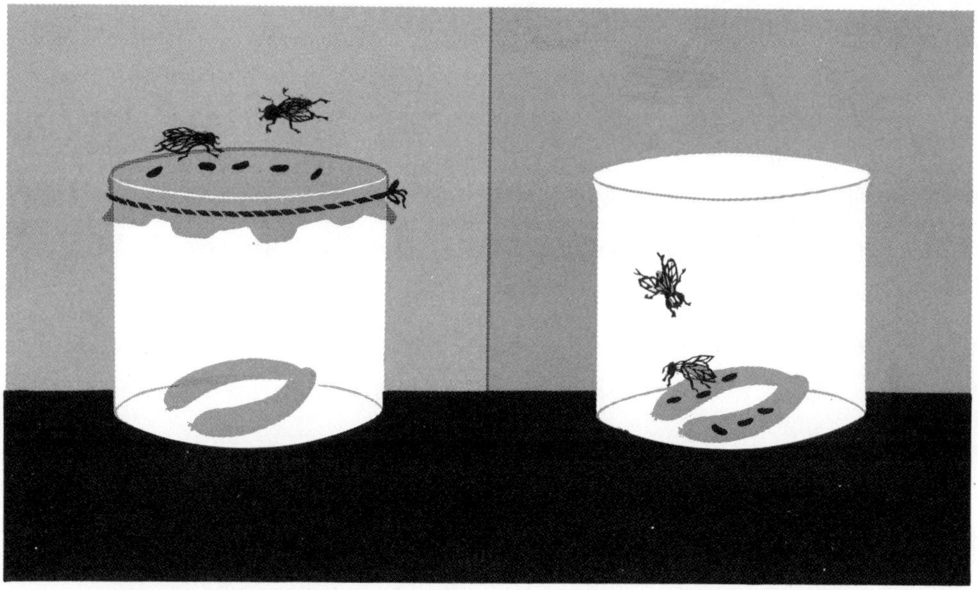

Redi's experiment helped to prove that living things are reproduced from other living things like themselves.

Soon, he found maggots on the uncovered meat. The covered meat was free of maggots.

This was very strange. Where had the maggots on the uncovered meat come from, if not from the meat itself? And why were there no maggots on the covered meat?

Francesco Redi discovered the answer. He saw that flies could reach the uncovered meat and lay their eggs in it. The maggots then grew out of these eggs. Later, the maggots would become flies.

He also saw why the covered meat had no maggots. The flies could not reach the meat through the fine muslin covering the jars.

This was a splendid experiment. Francesco Redi proved that maggots do not generate in meat by themselves. They come from flies' eggs. And he saved housewives a great deal of worry; from this time on, all they had to do to prevent meat from spoiling too quickly was to keep it well covered and away from flies.

But this still did not explain how the tiny organisms appeared in the pepper water. The tiny sticks, or rods, that Leeuwenhoek and Hooke had seen could not have come from flies' eggs.

The problem was not solved until about two hundred years later, when the great French scientist Louis Pasteur performed an experiment which has become famous in the history of science.

## Pasteur's Discoveries

Pasteur used a special kind of glass flask which had a long curved neck. The neck was shaped rather like the letter S.

He put some broth in the flask, and boiled it until it steamed.

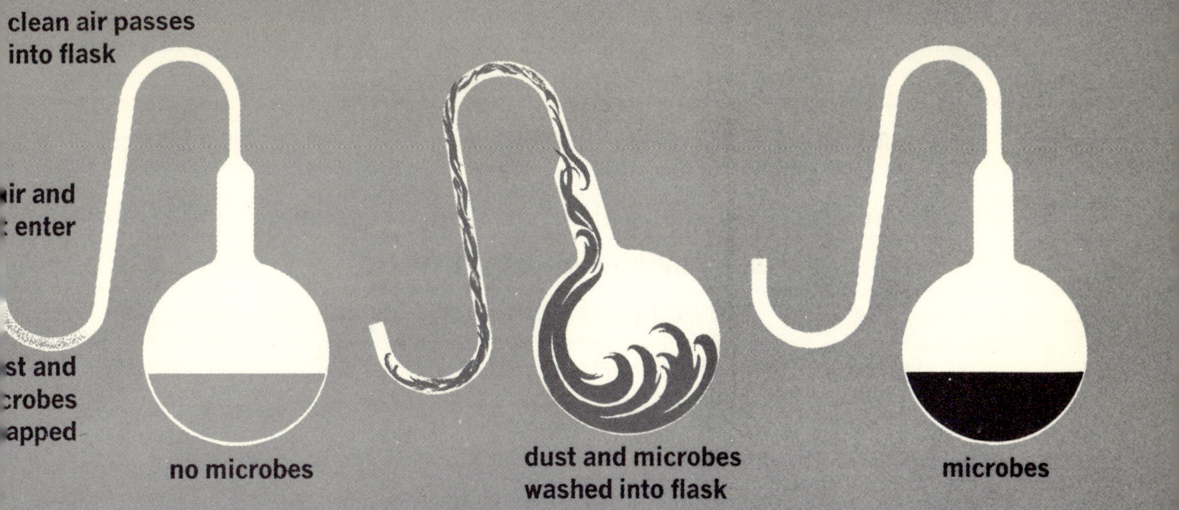

The great French scientist, Louis Pasteur (left), made many important discoveries. One of his experiments proved that germs come from germs.

In this way he killed any tiny organisms both in the broth and in the S-shaped neck.

He left the end of the neck open, so that air could reach the broth freely.

After he had boiled the broth, he waited for several days.

No living organisms appeared in the broth. It remained perfectly clear.

Then Pasteur shook the flask, so that the broth splashed into the S-shaped neck and trickled back into the flask.

Within a short time the broth became cloudy with living organisms.

Several important facts were proved by this experiment.

First, Pasteur proved that spontaneous generation did not take place in the broth, since it remained perfectly clear for several days after he boiled it.

He also proved that spontaneous generation did not take place in the air, since air could reach the broth freely through the S-shaped neck.

But tiny living organisms might be *carried* through the air by air currents or on particles of dust.

And this, Pasteur showed, was precisely what happened in his experiment.

Tiny living organisms—"germs," as he called them—were carried through the air into the neck of the flask.

But once they were inside the neck, the germs were trapped in the S-shaped bend.

There they remained, until Pasteur shook the flask and washed them into the broth.

Then the germs began to multiply, until the broth was cloudy with them. So, the mystery was solved. Germs do not come into existence by spontaneous generation. Germs come from germs. All living things come into existence by reproduction from living things like themselves.

We owe an immense debt to these men who peered through microscopes and tried to understand the puzzling things they saw. By their scientific curiosity, and by their hard work, they increased beyond measure the happiness and the health of the human race. Let us count up some of the things they accomplished for us.

Before Pasteur's time, hospitals were dirty and dangerous. Operations were to be dreaded. Doctors had almost no idea how infections started or how they spread.

Pasteur showed that bacteria can be carried in the

air, and that they can come only from bacteria. Most of these organisms cause us little trouble, normally; but if they enter an open wound they may multiply rapidly, and then they can cause serious illness.

A great English surgeon named Joseph Lister followed up Pasteur's work by introducing the principles of antiseptic surgery. Hospitals are infinitely

In modern hospitals every care is taken to protect patients from harmful bacteria. In this operating room, air is 99.9 per cent free of bacteria.

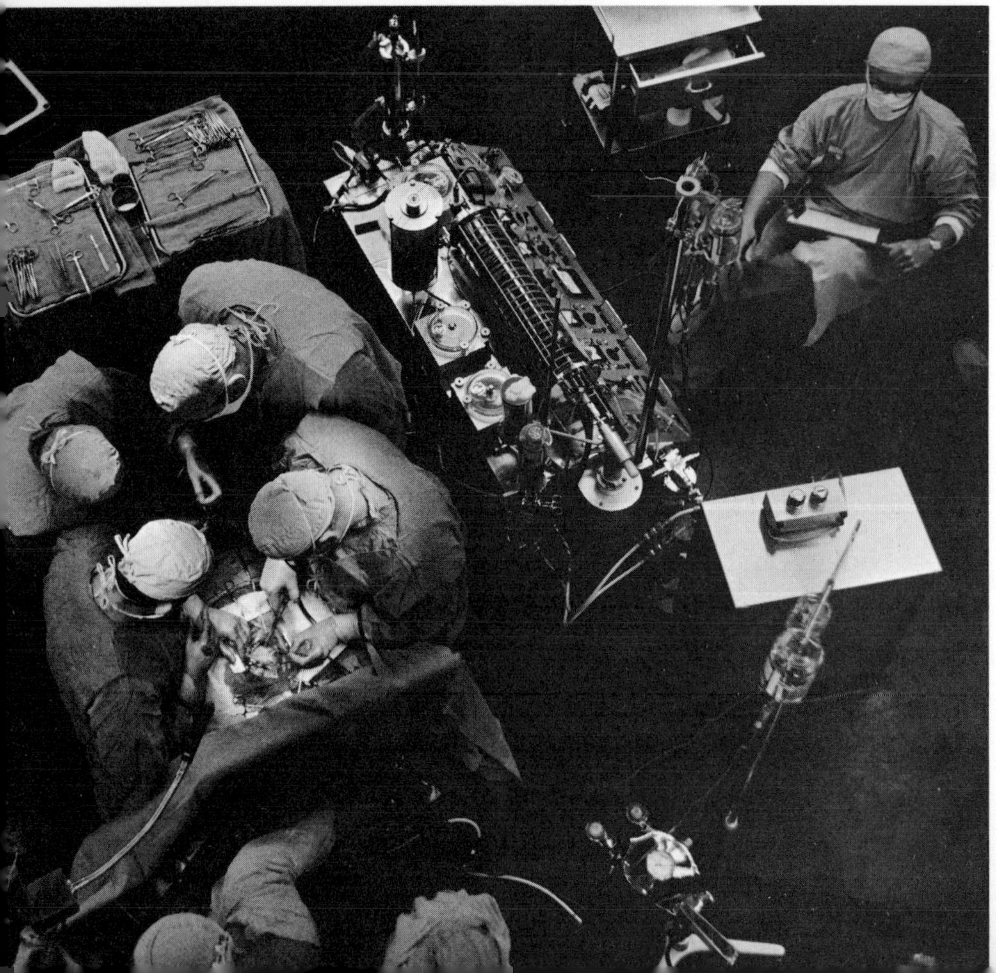

safer now because of Pasteur and Lister and the scientists who developed their ideas.

Soldiers wounded in battle often died because of infection by bacteria. The lives of countless soldiers were saved as a result of Pasteur's discoveries.

Farmers all over the world were helped, because the work of Pasteur enabled them to control terrible diseases which ravaged their livestock.

A cure was found for rabies, a disease transmitted by the bite of mad dogs, which until Pasteur's time had always been fatal.

Doctors, following in Pasteur's footsteps, learned how to control some of the fearful epidemics which, in the past, had killed millions of people.

## The Cell Theory

Scientists were also learning more about Hooke's discovery: cells.

Step by step, the mysteries of the cell were uncovered. Here, very briefly, are some of the more important of these steps.

In 1824, a French scientist named Dutrochet suggested, for the first time, that all living things are composed of cells.

In 1831, an English scientist named Robert Brown found that in each of the cells of some orchids he was studying there was a small spot, darker than the rest of the cell. He called this spot the NUCLEUS.

In 1839, two German scientists, Schleiden and Schwann, published a cell theory similar to Dutrochet's. This was the result of their own research, however, and it was quickly accepted by scientists everywhere, although some of their ideas were later shown to be incorrect.

Twenty years later, a German doctor named Rudolf Virchow summed up, in an impressive Latin phrase, what the work of these scientists had proved: *Omnis cellula e cellula,* "all cells come from cells."

Today, scientists make one important exception to this rule: life, in its simplest form, must have begun by spontaneous generation billions of years ago. But, scientists point out, the earth was then very different from the earth as it is now, and in those very special conditions spontaneous generation was possible.

Biology, the science of life, is today based on the study of the cell. Many of the deepest secrets of nature are locked in the tiny cell, and, as each day passes, scientists are coming a little closer to understanding these complicated mysteries.

# PART THREE

# Animals of One Cell and Animals of Many Cells

*Now we are going to look at several members of the animal kingdom: some one-celled animals; the tiny hydra which you can find in almost any pond; the remarkable earthworm; and the most complex creature of all, man. We will see how they are constructed, how they move, how they get their food, how they are nourished by their food, and how they reproduce.*

*We will see, too, that although they are very different, they yet have much in common. Even the simplest of them are studied carefully by scientists, because they provide important insights into the ways living things are formed and the ways they behave.*

# Amoeba and Paramecium

In all probability, one of the "animalcules" that Leeuwenhoek saw through his microscope was a little creature known to us now as Amoeba proteus.

AMOEBA comes from a Greek word meaning "change." And, in Greek mythology, Proteus was a sea god who could take on any shape. This is one of the fascinating things about the amoeba—it changes its shape as you watch it.

There are a number of different kinds of amoebas.

Animal life takes many forms, including the jellyfish shown here. But all, from amoeba to man, have certain problems in common.

Some are the cause of illness. Some, like Amoeba proteus, are harmless.

Amoeba proteus lives in ponds. You can catch it by using a glass jar and scooping up some of the muddy water at the bottom of a pond. When the mud settles in the jar and the water becomes clear, you will see many tiny organisms; and one of these might very possibly be an amoeba. You can just see it with the naked eye.

Let us suppose that you have caught one, and that you have a microscope so that you can examine it closely.

Perhaps the first thing you will notice is that it consists of a single cell. The amoeba belongs to the Protozoa—the "first animals," which came into existence more than a billion years ago.

The next thing you may notice is that the amoeba appears to be merely a formless blob of jelly.

However, if you look very carefully, you will see that there seems to be a very thin, clear, flexible film around the amoeba. This is a delicate envelope which serves to hold the amoeba together. It is called the CELL MEMBRANE.

The watery jelly inside the amoeba is called CYTO-

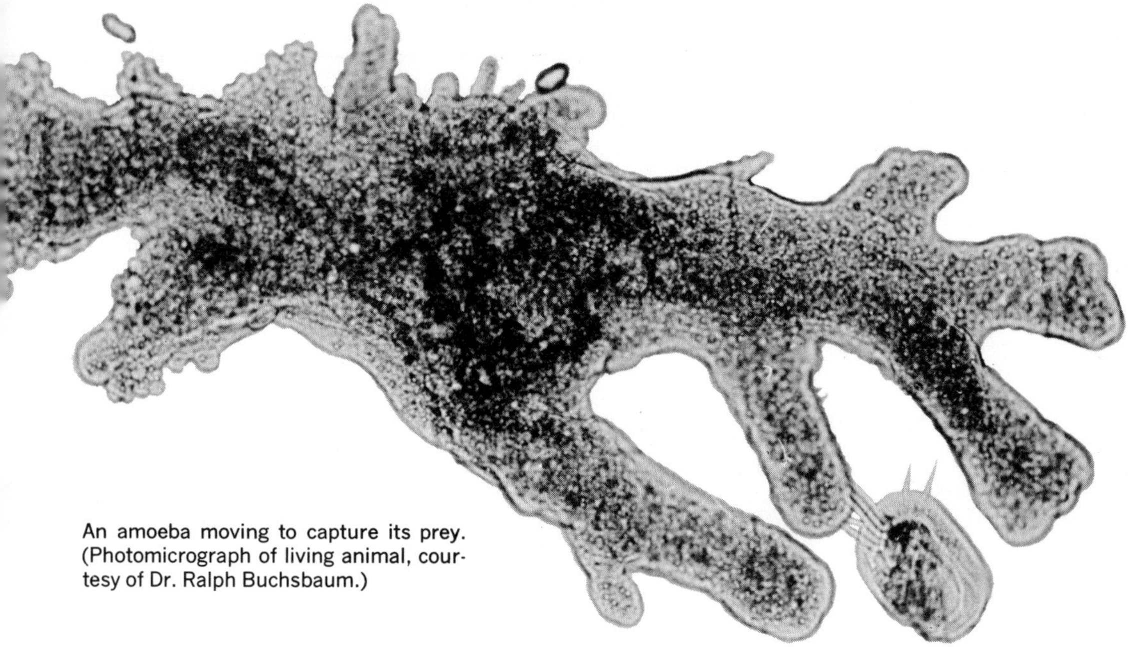

An amoeba moving to capture its prey. (Photomicrograph of living animal, courtesy of Dr. Ralph Buchsbaum.)

PLASM. *Cyto* means "cell"; *plasm* means "substance." There are some bubbles in it, called VACUOLES; some little gray spots, called GRANULES; and a round dark area, called the NUCLEUS.

That is all. A living creature could hardly be any simpler.

Yet it is one of the most remarkable animals in the world.

As you watch it you will see that it moves in a peculiar way. It seems to flow. One part of itself reaches out, and the rest of the body follows.

The part that reaches out is called a PSEUDOPO-

DIUM, which means "a false foot." But this is a misleading name. The amoeba has no limbs at all, false or real.

Scientists are not sure what happens when the amoeba moves. According to one theory, the amoeba somehow squeezes its cytoplasm at one end, rather as you squeeze a tube of toothpaste; and then the whole of the amoeba's body moves forward.

When the amoeba finds a particle of food, another strange thing happens. It has no mouth, so it pushes out one or more pseudopodia and wraps itself around the food, forming a little bubble in which the food is trapped.

This bubble is called a FOOD VACUOLE, and it acts as a sort of stomach. The vacuole moves through the cytoplasm of the amoeba while juices enter and digest the food. Then molecules of the substances which the amoeba needs, such as amino acids, move out of the bubble into the cytoplasm. Waste substances stay in the bubble and are carried outside the amoeba, where the bubble bursts in the water so that the wastes drift away.

This is a very striking fact. Although the food vacuole is inside the amoeba, the food itself remains inside the vacuole. Therefore the food does not actually come into contact with the cytoplasm of the amoeba until it is thoroughly digested. Only then do the molecules of nourishing substances move out of the vacuole into the amoeba's cytoplasm.

The same happens when you, too, eat something. The food remains within your digestive tract while it is being digested. In the digestive tract the food is not actually in contact with the cells of your body. The reason is simple: undigested food would be highly dangerous if it entered the blood stream. Before food can leave the digestive tract and be carried all over your body, it is broken down into the various kinds of molecules your body needs.

There are also one or two bubbles of another sort inside the amoeba. These are called CONTRACTILE VACUOLES. They collect any excess water in the amoeba's body. This water is then discharged outside the cell.

Tiny as it is, the one-celled amoeba has many things in common with more complex forms of life. Because it has no brain, it cannot be said to think. Because it has no nervous system, it cannot be said to feel. Yet if it is touched gently with the point of a needle, it backs away. It is sensitive to heat and cold. It moves from strong light into shade.

Scientists describe these as REACTIONS TO STIMULI. More complicated animals, including human beings, react to stimuli in much the same way.

## Reproduction of the Amoeba

The manner in which the amoeba reproduces itself is called FISSION.

If you watched this under a microscope, you would see that it happens in several distinct stages.

First, the amoeba pulls in all its pseudopodia. Its shape becomes more or less the shape of a ball.

Then the middle of the one-celled animal becomes narrower, as if it were being nipped by an invisible belt.

At the same time, changes take place in the dark spot inside the amoeba—the nucleus. Soon, the nucleus divides into two equal parts. One part goes to one end of the amoeba, and the other part goes to the other end.

Then the narrow part in the middle becomes narrower and narrower, until finally the amoeba is nipped completely into two equal parts, each containing its own nucleus.

Now there are two amoebas where there was only one before.

Neither of them is the "parent" amoeba. They are both "daughter" amoebas, and they are exactly alike.

Then each may divide again. Now the original amoeba exists as four amoebas, all exactly alike.

Because of the way it reproduces, scientists have called the amoeba an immortal animal. Some scientists have pointed out that all the amoebas in a pond may, in fact, be the same amoeba existing in an enormous number of separate bodies!

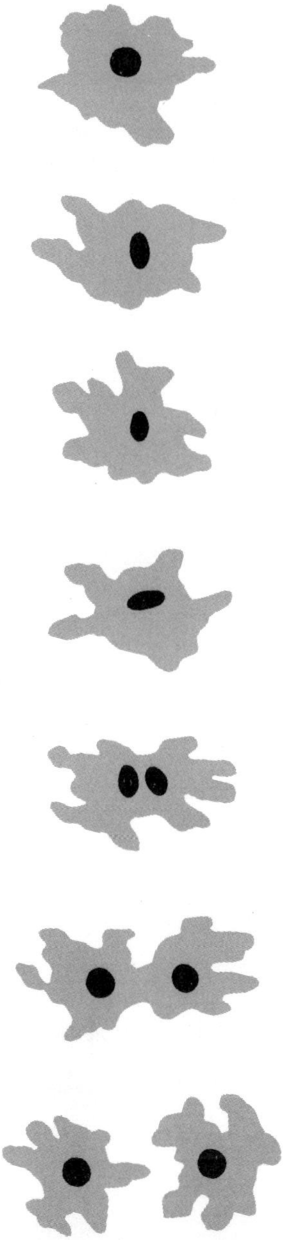

By the process of fission, the amoeba becomes two new amoebas.

## Paramecium

Another interesting one-celled animal is the paramecium. Its name comes from a Greek word which means "oblong." It, too, lives in ponds. It is so tiny that even in a small pond there may be more paramecia than there are human beings in the whole world.

The outer envelope of the paramecium, thicker and firmer than that of the amoeba, is called the PELLICLE. Covering the pellicle are rows of tiny hairs called CILIA. These work like tiny oars rowing a boat. Beating with a wavelike motion, they enable the paramecium to swim in any direction, even backward.

The paramecium does not engulf its food as the amoeba does. In its body there is a sort of funnel called the ORAL GROOVE, lined with strong cilia that drive particles of food down it. The oral groove might be compared to a human being's ESOPHAGUS—the tube leading from the mouth to the stomach.

At the bottom of the oral groove a little vacuole forms to collect the food particles.

When enough food has entered the vacuole, it breaks away and begins a journey that takes it al-

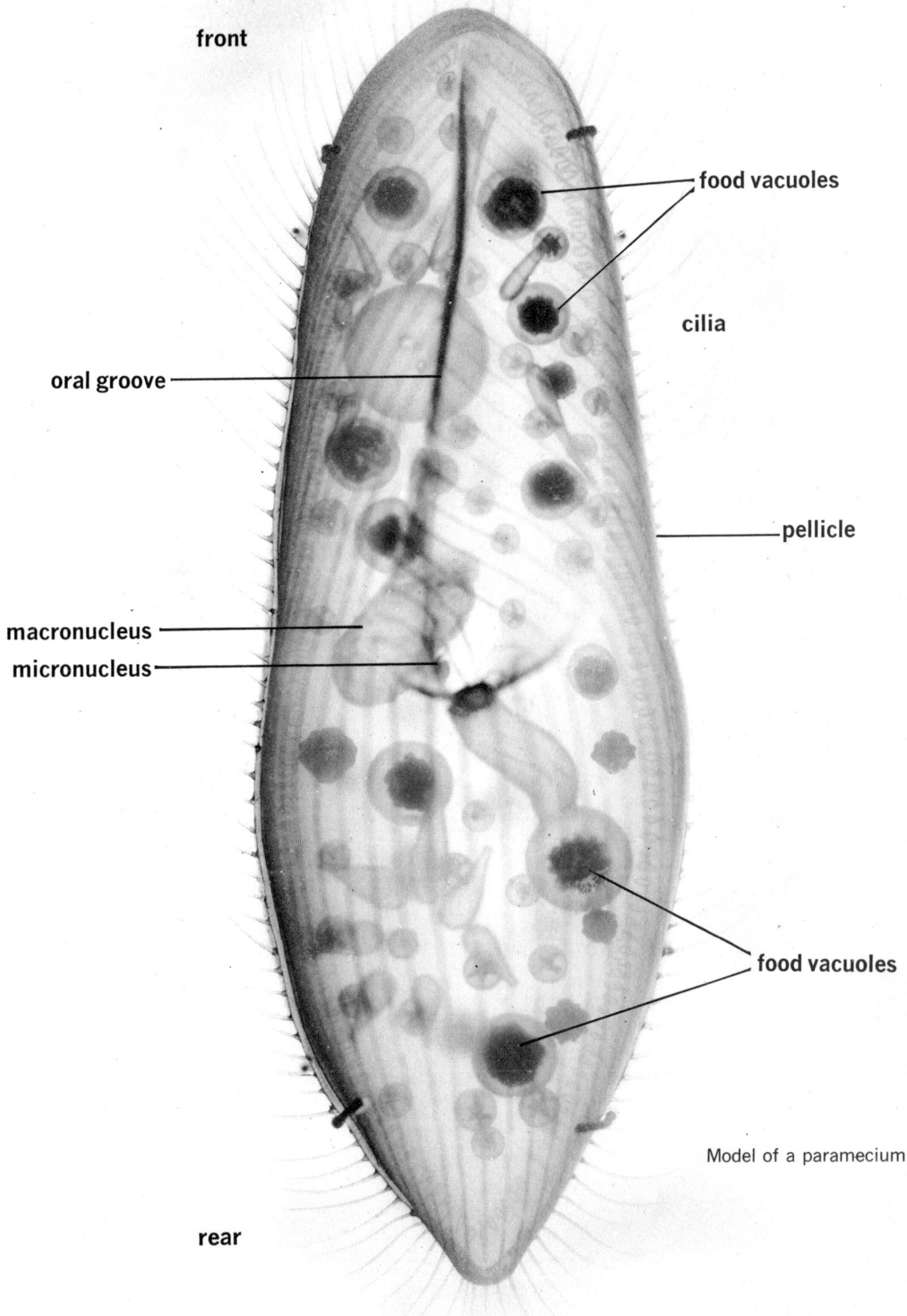


Model of a paramecium.

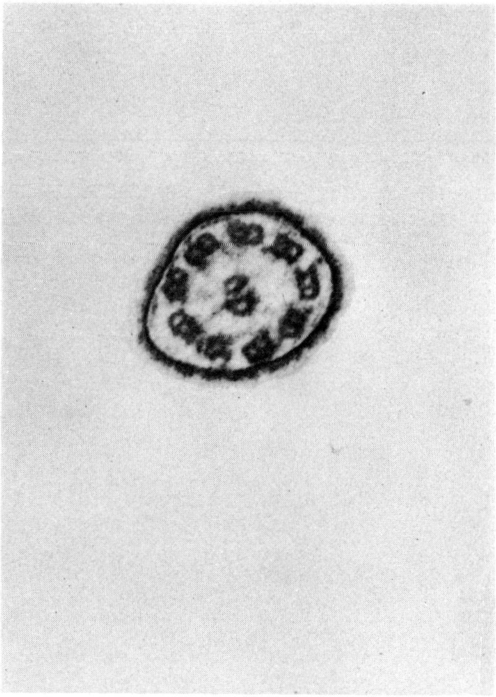

Cilium of a paramecium, shown in cross-section. It has been magnified 125,000 times.

most all the way around the cytoplasm of the paramecium, and the food is digested just as it is in the amoeba. Finally, the food wastes, still in their little bubble, are discharged at a special point just below the oral groove, called the ANAL PORE.

When we examine the paramecium carefully, we realize how complicated a tiny one-celled animal can be. Even the little cilia on its body are constructed in a very complex way. If you examined the end of one of these cilia through an electron microscope you would see that it is composed of two center rods, surrounded by a circle of nine double rods. All living things, with a few exceptions such as the amoeba, have cilia similar to those of the paramecium. For example, there are cilia lining your breathing passages, from the inside of your nose to your lungs. Their purpose is to trap, and sweep up and out of your body, harmful particles of dust and bacteria that might have entered from the air.

## Reproduction of the Paramecium

The paramecium reproduces in two different ways. One way is by fission. This is rather like the way the amoeba reproduces, although there is one striking difference.

Look at the model of the paramecium again. Notice how complicated it is compared to an amoeba. For example, there is the oral groove. There is not a single nucleus, but two. Furthermore, the paramecium has a definite shape: one end is more pointed than the other.

This complicated construction raises many questions. If the paramecium divides in the same way as the amoeba, simply by nipping across the middle, will one of the daughter cells have a pointed end and the other a blunt end? Will each daughter cell have half of the oral groove? And what will happen to the two nuclei?

Let us see what actually happens when the paramecium divides.

First, the oral groove becomes fainter and fainter, until it can no longer be seen. The smaller nucleus, called the MICRONUCLEUS, seems to stretch out more and more, until it divides into two halves, each half at opposite ends of the cell. The larger nucleus, called the MACRONUCLEUS, divides in two, and each half moves close to each half of the micronucleus.

Then, as the middle of the cell becomes pinched in, a new oral groove forms in the top half of the cell, and another oral groove forms in the bottom half of the cell. At the same time a new contractile vacuole forms in each half. Now the cell pinches in more and more, until it separates into two cells, each one a complete paramecium.

The second way the paramecium reproduces is called CONJUGATION. It involves two paramecia.

Conjugation is far more complex than fission, and it happens less frequently. Some scientists who wanted to make a film of conjugation had to wait months and months for it to occur among the thousands of paramecia in their laboratory.

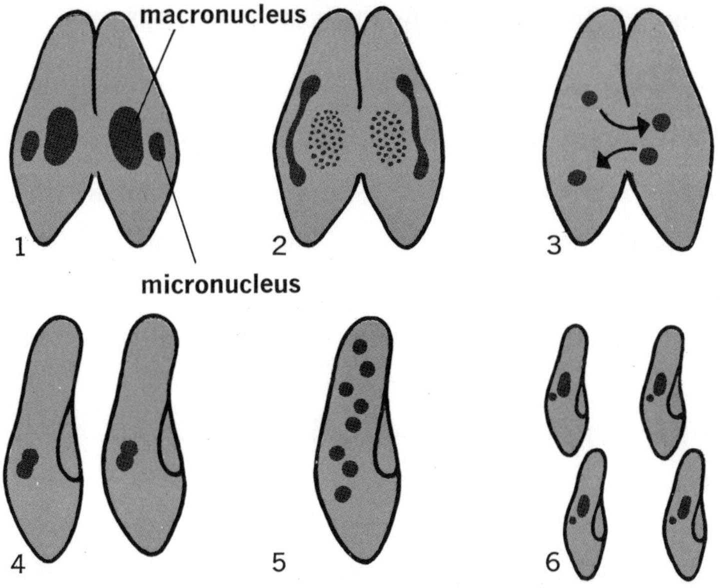


When paramecia reproduce by conjugation, the new paramecia are slightly different from each parent.

(1) It begins when two paramecia join together side by side for a brief period of time.

(2) The macronucleus appears to break down, and disappears into the cytoplasm of each cell.

Two divisions take place in the micronucleus of each paramecium, so that each has four micronuclei.

Then three of the micronuclei in each cell disappear, and the one that is left divides again.

(3) Now comes the most important part of conjugation. Each of the paramecia *exchanges* one of its micronuclei.

Thus, each has one of its own and one it has received from the other paramecium. This is the real purpose of the cells joining together—to *pass* a micronucleus, in a special form, to the other cell and to *receive* one from the other cell.

(4) The two micronuclei in each cell now fuse together.

When this occurs, the cells are said to be FERTILIZED.

(5–6) The two paramecia separate and go their own ways. After more divisions, and the formation of a new macronucleus, each cell is ready to divide in the simpler way, by fission.

Once the two paramecia have exchanged micronuclei, each is different from what it was before the exchange took place. If paramecia always reproduced by fission, the generations that followed would all be exactly alike. But as a result of conjugation there are slight differences among the generations of paramecia that follow.

How does this help paramecia?

Imagine millions of these tiny animals living in a small pond. Imagine that the summer has come, and the weather is unusually warm. Perhaps the water in the pond becomes too warm for most of the paramecia. If they were all alike, they might all die. But since they are not all exactly alike, some of them may be able to tolerate higher temperatures than others. These, therefore, will go on living. So, differences among paramecia enable them to adapt to new living conditions, and thus the species survives.

# Hydra

Altogether there are more than 15,000 different kinds of one-celled Protozoa. If we could study them here in more detail, you might be surprised at how many strange forms a tiny one-celled animal can take.

One, called Vorticella, is like a bell on a long stalk. Another, called Stentor, is shaped like a trumpet. Some forms have a delicate structure of silica. Others have a skeleton of a chalky substance.

But, like the paramecium, each kind of one-celled

Among the many kinds of one-celled animals are the Foraminifera. When they die, their shells (here magnified 350 times) fall to the bottom of the sea, where they become chalk.

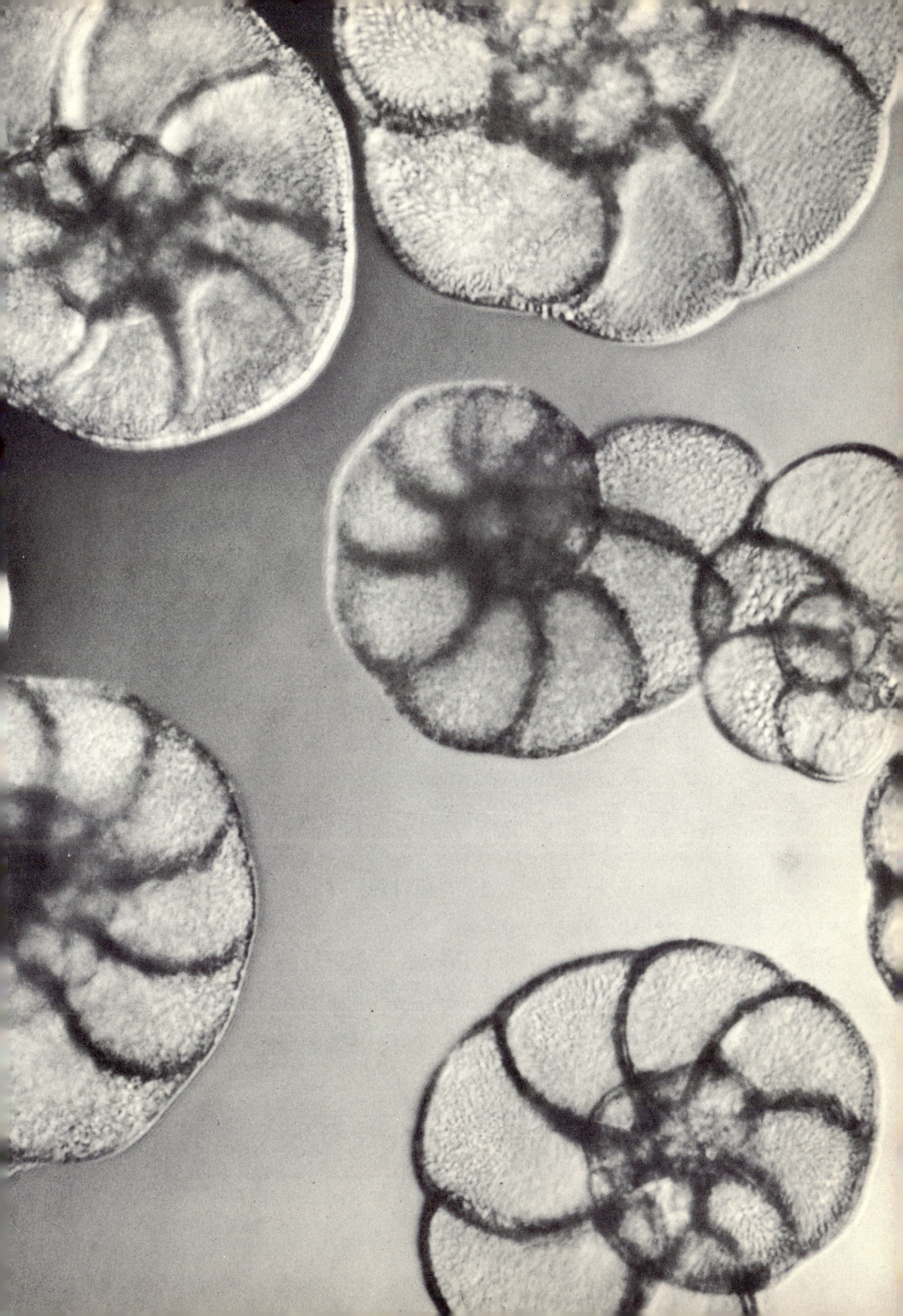

animal must obtain food, digest the food, pass the food around its body, obtain oxygen, expel wastes, reproduce itself, move around. The single cell must be able to carry out all these activities.

## Multi-celled Animals

In animals composed of many cells, certain cells can do different things. The cells are said to SPECIALIZE. Some specialize in movement, some in obtaining oxygen, some in getting rid of wastes. Some make chemicals that the animal needs. Some specialize in reproduction. In this way they all contribute something to benefit the multi-celled animal, and in doing so they benefit themselves.

Both kinds of animals, one-celled and multi-celled, have advantages and disadvantages.

For example, it is rather simple for a single-celled animal like the paramecium to supply itself with the nourishment it needs. Its cilia sweep food particles down the oral groove. Then a food vacuole carries the food particles around the paramecium's cytoplasm, and the digested food substances move into the cytoplasm. Then the wastes are neatly expelled outside the cell.

Now think of an animal composed of millions or billions of cells. Many of these cells will be deep inside the animal. How will food reach these cells? Obviously, food must be carried to them somehow. And how can these cells get rid of their wastes? The wastes must somehow be carried away, to be discharged outside the animal's body.

So a multi-celled animal must have what scientists call a SYSTEM OF TRANSPORTATION to carry food and oxygen all over its body, and to carry off waste substances.

The multi-celled animal has problems, therefore, that the one-celled animal does not have.

But the multi-celled animal also has many advantages. It can be much bigger and much stronger than any one-celled animal; a minnow is a huge giant compared to a paramecium. Furthermore, if a one-celled animal is injured—and, particularly, if its nucleus is damaged—it will probably die. But a many-celled animal can suffer injuries to a number of its cells and still go on living.

## The Hydra's Specialized Cells

One of the simplest multi-celled animals is the

hydra. In Greek mythology the hydra was a huge, snakelike monster with nine heads. It was so fearsome that the mighty Hercules was given the task of slaying it. This was a difficult problem, even for Hercules, because as soon as one of the hydra's heads was cut off, two more grew to replace it.

Our hydra is not in the least bit fearsome. It is not at all like a snake. And when you find it in a pond you need a magnifying glass to see it clearly, because it is scarcely a quarter of an inch long. It consists of about 100,000 cells.

But the hydra is like its namesake in one way. If its "head"—or, rather, the top part of its body—is cut off, a new top part will soon grow. And even if it is cut into small pieces, each piece may grow into a complete hydra.

The hydra is related to the corals (which build coral reefs), sea anemones, and jellyfish. Its body is like a long slender vase, closed at the bottom but open at the top. This opening is called the mouth, and it is surrounded by six or eight tentacles, which are extensions of the body.

It moves, very slowly, in several ways. It can creep along the bottom of a pond. Or it can float on a little bubble that forms at the closed end of

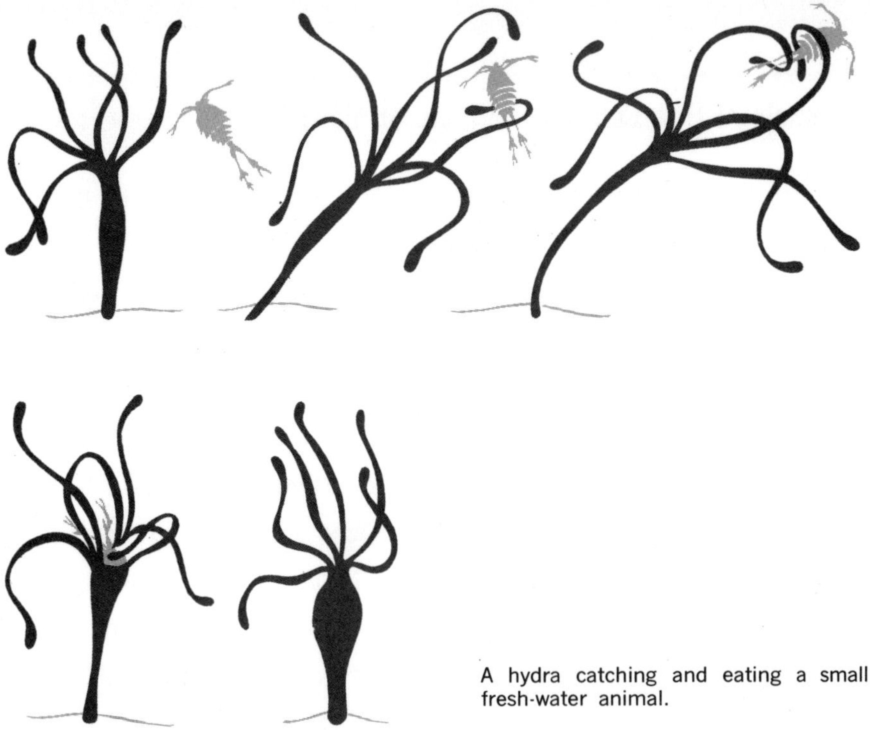

A hydra catching and eating a small fresh-water animal.

its body. Or, sometimes, it takes several slow somersaults, like a circus clown.

When it finds a suitable rock or plant, it attaches itself by spreading out the closed end of its body into a sort of foot. There it remains, with its tentacles extended, waiting for some small animal like a water flea to come close.

Then, if the unsuspecting water flea happens to touch a tentacle, it is held fast, just as if it had been caught on a piece of flypaper. No matter how hard it struggles, it cannot get away. Slowly, the tentacle carries the water flea toward the hydra's mouth; the mouth opens wide; and the water flea passes into the hydra's body.

This is strange, because the hydra does not have any sticky material on its tentacles. Why is it that the water flea appears to be held so tightly?

When we examine the hydra's tentacles under a microscope, we can understand what happens. On the outside of each tentacle there are hundreds of special cells called STINGING CELLS. Coiled within each stinging cell is a hollow thread, or filament, attached to a sac of poison. As soon as the water flea touches a tentacle, dozens of the hollow threads explode out of the stinging cells and pierce the water flea like harpoons. At the same time, poison is injected through the hollow threads into the water flea, which cannot possibly free itself.

The hydra cannot harm human beings; but some of the jellyfish which are related to it have poisonous stinging cells that can be very painful, and even dangerous. This explains why it is not wise to swim in the sea if there are many jellyfish floating in the water.

The stinging cells are only one kind of special cell possessed by the hydra. If we continue to examine this remarkable animal through a microscope we will see other kinds.

The inside of the hydra's body is like a sac. The walls of this sac are made of two layers of cells, with a thin layer of a jelly-like substance between them.

The outer layer serves to protect the hydra, in the same way that your skin protects you. The stinging cells are in the outer layer.

The inner layer consists of several different kinds of cells. MUCUS CELLS, near the mouth, keep the passage slippery so that food will pass through easily. GLAND CELLS release juices which begin to digest the food. FLAGELLATED CELLS keep the food materials circulating through the sac, by movements of their long filaments.

But only part of the process of digestion takes place in the sac. When the food has been broken into sufficiently small chunks, the cells absorb it in much the same way that the amoeba gets its food, by bulging around the particles and enclosing them in vacuoles. Then the digestion of the food is completed inside the cell. There is no need for a special system of transportation since the particles of food can reach all the cells without difficulty.

Because there are only two layers of cells, oxygen

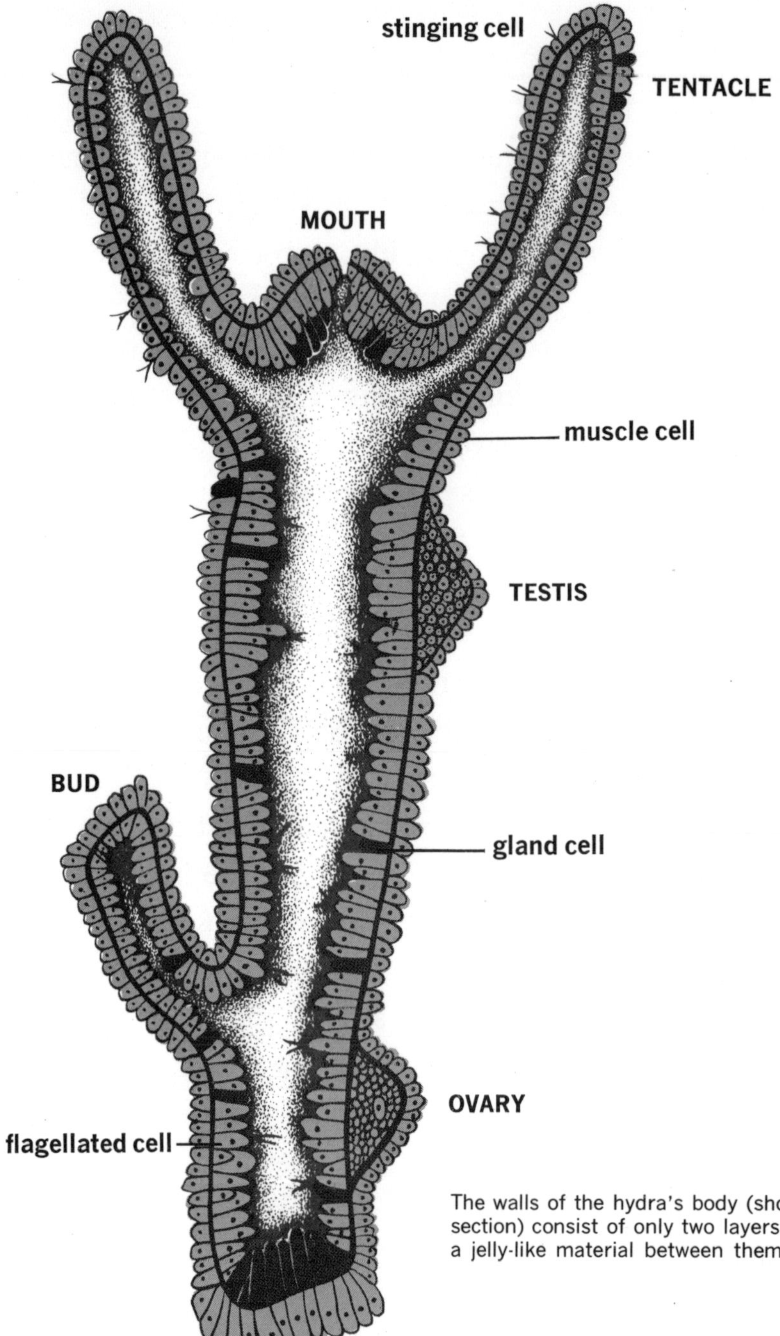


The walls of the hydra's body (shown in cross-section) consist of only two layers of cells with a jelly-like material between them.

from the surrounding water can easily reach all the cells in the hydra's body, and carbon dioxide can easily pass out. But because the hydra is constructed like a vase, with one end closed, undigested food particles must pass out through the same opening by which the food entered, the mouth.

## The Nervous System of the Hydra

The hydra does not have a brain, so it cannot think. How does it become aware that a water flea has touched one of its tentacles? And how is it able to move from place to place?

It can move because many of its cells are able to contract, rather like the muscles of your body. If you contract the biceps muscle of your upper arm, your forearm is pulled up. In the same way the contraction of the hydra's cells enable it to shorten and bend its body so that it can propel itself slowly through the water, and also move its tentacles.

Your muscles contract when an impulse reaches them through a nerve or a number of nerves. The hydra has a complicated network of nerves over its body and tentacles. Across this network pass the impulses which bring about movement. When a

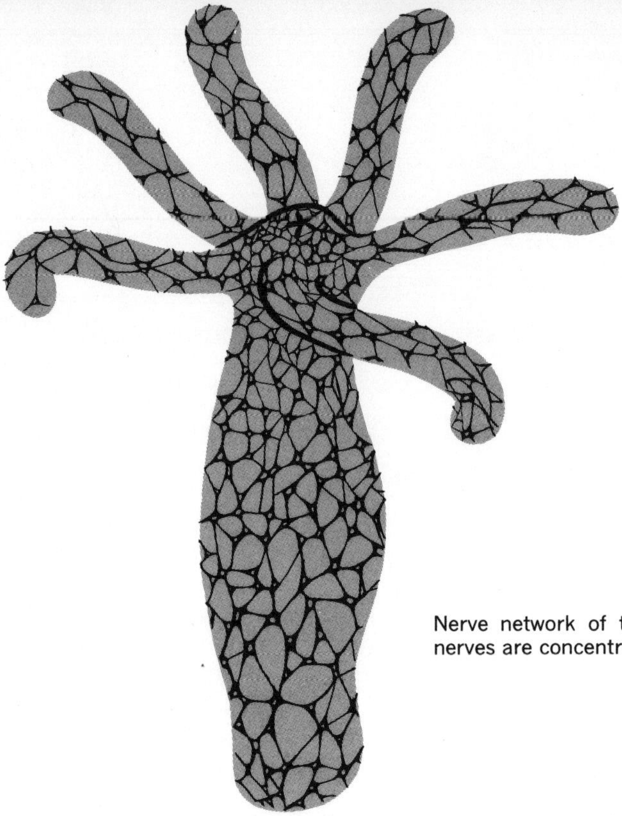

Nerve network of the hydra. Notice how the nerves are concentrated near the mouth.

water flea touches a tentacle, nerves are alerted. Then impulses quickly pass along the nerves to the batteries of stinging cells, and the coiled harpoon-like stings are released.

## Reproduction of the Hydra

We saw in the last chapter the two ways in which paramecia can reproduce. Reproduction by fission is sometimes called ASEXUAL, meaning "nonsexual." The cell simply divides, forming two cells that are exactly alike.

The second way is sometimes called SEXUAL REPRODUCTION. Two paramecia join together, or conjugate, and exchange nuclei. Then they separate; and later, when they divide by fission, the daughter cells are slightly different from the parent cell.

The hydra, also, can reproduce in two ways, asexual and sexual. But both ways are quite different from those of the paramecium.

The hydra's way of reproducing asexually is by BUDDING.

The bud begins as a small swelling on the side of the hydra's body. The bud is hollow (like the hydra's body), and it grows out rather like the finger of a glove.

Soon the bud develops a mouth and tentacles, and it is able to catch its own food. When there are several buds growing on the parent hydra's body, all with tentacles and all hungrily trying to get food, there is quite a lot of confusion. But it is not long before each young hydra separates from the parent and goes off to live its own life.

The hydras usually reproduce sexually in the autumn.

Again, small swellings appear on the side of each

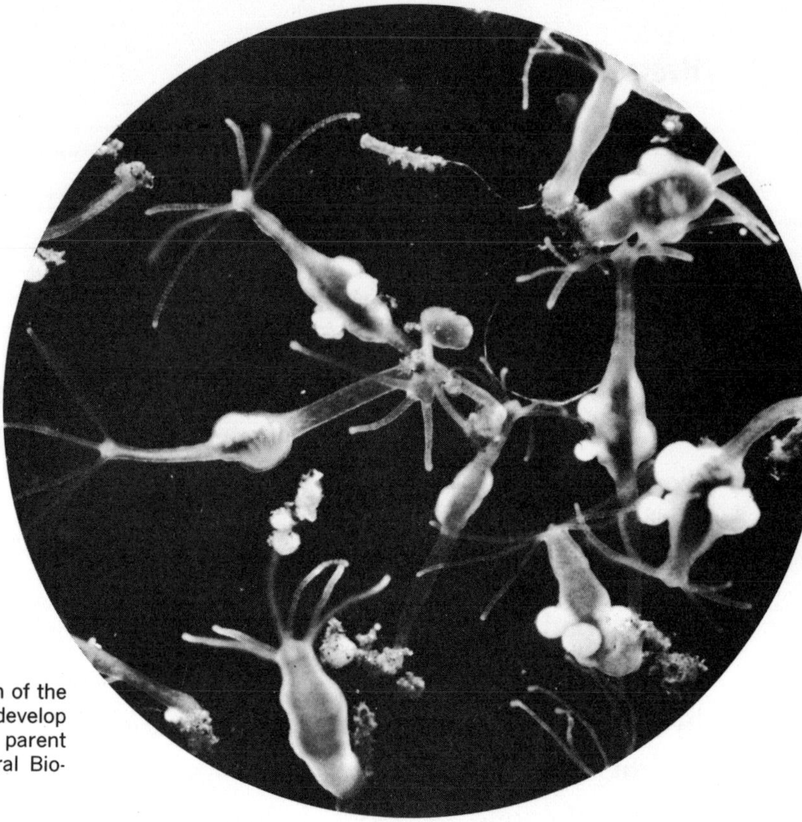

During sexual reproduction of the hydra, fertilized egg cells develop while still attached to the parent hydra. (Courtesy of General Biological Supply House).

hydra's body. These are not buds, though. They are two different kinds of organs in which special cells are produced.

One kind of organ is called an OVARY. This is the female organ, and it produces one cell at a time —an OVUM, or egg cell.

The other kind of organ is called a TESTIS. This is the male organ. It produces a considerable number of cells called SPERMS.

The hydras do not come together, as paramecia do in conjugation. The sperms are discharged into the water from the testis. Each sperm consists of a small oval-shaped nucleus with a sharp tip in front and a long thin tail behind. The tail lashes violently, carrying the sperm through the water.

The egg cell is not discharged into the water. It remains attached to the hydra.

The sperms can stay alive for three days. The egg cell stays alive for only about one day.

If a sperm reaches an egg cell, the sharp tip penetrates the egg cell, and the long thin tail drops off. Then the nucleus of the sperm and the nucleus of the egg cell combine, and the egg is now fertilized.

It proceeds to split into two cells. But these do not separate. They remain attached to each other. They split again, into four cells, then into eight, and soon they take the form of a hollow ball consisting of a single layer of cells. This is called the BLASTULA, which means "a little sprout" or "shoot."

The cells continue to divide, and fill the hollow of the blastula. Now it is called a GASTRULA, which means "little stomach," although no stomach has been formed.

A protective shell forms around the gastrula; and at last it separates from the parent hydra and falls to the bottom of the pond, remaining there through the winter. During this time the cells inside the gastrula form the inner layer of the animal, and its tentacles grow. Then, in the spring, the little hydra comes to the surface of the pond and soon, if it is lucky, it has caught its first water flea.

The hydra is unique in many ways. It is made of only seven different kinds of cells. Its body is composed of only two layers. More complex animals are built of very many different kinds of cells, and they are composed of three layers.

But the sperms of the hydra are similar to the sperms of all more complex animals, including human beings. The sperms all have a pointed head, to penetrate the egg cell, and a long tail which enables them to swim quite speedily (considering their tiny size) in search of an egg cell.

Now, the sperms of the hydra and the sperms of animals like fish have no difficulty swimming in the water in which the parent animals normally live.

But what happens when the sperms are not in a liquid?

They can move only with difficulty. Sperms are

more or less helpless when they are out of a liquid.

This raises a serious problem.

How can the sperms find and fertilize the egg cells of animals that live on the land?

The answer is: the sperms must be passed from the male directly into the body of the female. We will see more clearly how this happens in the next chapters.

# The Remarkable Earthworm

Few people except farmers, fishermen, and biologists seem to care very much about the earthworm.

This is a pity. It is really such a remarkable creature that scientists study it in great detail.

As its name implies, the earthworm lives in the ground. It is long and tubular. Its color is red-brown or purple-brown. It has no eyes, no ears, no feet. Its front is thicker and more pointed than its tail.

The earthworm is of great importance to farmers—and therefore to all of us—because by burrowing in the earth it turns the soil over, allowing air and moisture to penetrate below the surface. As a result the soil is made more fertile, and plants thrive. Scientists have calculated that in an acre of farmland there may be more than a million earthworms living near the surface, and even more deeper below. If there are no earthworms in the soil it becomes lumpy and hard, and plants have difficulty growing.

## How the Earthworm Moves

The body of the earthworm is encircled by what appear to be little rings. These tell us how the animal is constructed. It is not a simple continuous tube. It is composed of segments. A big earthworm may have nearly two hundred segments.

It is not the only animal to be constructed in this way. All animals more complex than the earthworm (with only a few exceptions, such as oysters and squid) are segmented. All insects are segmented. So are all animals with backbones, including human beings. (The segments of your body are marked off by the vertebrae down your spine and by your ribs.)

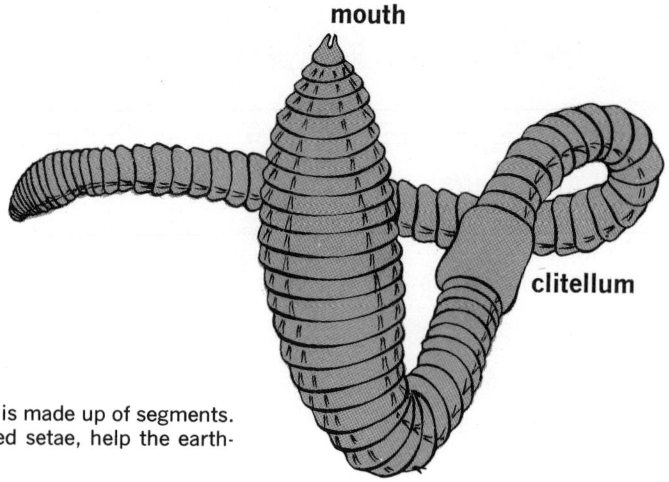


The earthworm's body is made up of segments. The little bristles, called setae, help the earthworm to move.

Protruding from each segment of the earthworm are four pairs of bristles called SETAE, which act like little walking sticks. Around the body is a layer of circular muscle; beneath this is a thick layer of muscle running the length of the body. When the earthworm moves, it first compresses the circular muscle, digging into the ground the setae on the rear portion of its body. This has the effect of making its body long and thin, and the front part is pushed forward. Next, it compresses the long muscles, making its body thick and digging in with its front setae, so that the rear part is pulled forward. This is sometimes compared by scientists to the action of an accordion.

Like more complex animals, the earthworm has a

digestive system, a system for transporting its food to all the cells of its body, a system for carrying away wastes, a nervous system, and a reproductive system. It does not have a bony skeleton, as we have; and it does not have a special breathing system like our lungs.

## How the Earthworm Digests Its Food

The body of the hydra, as we have seen, is like a sac, with one opening only, at the top. Through this single opening, food enters and wastes are also discharged.

The earthworm has a digestive system that is a great improvement over the hydra's. Its digestive tract extends all the way through its body, like a tube within a tube. One great advantage of this arrangement is that different sections of the tube can perform different tasks.

The earthworm's food consists of small pieces of plants and tiny organisms that it finds in the earth. It sucks the food in by means of strong muscles in its PHARYNX or throat. These muscles act like a pump; and at the same time that particles of food

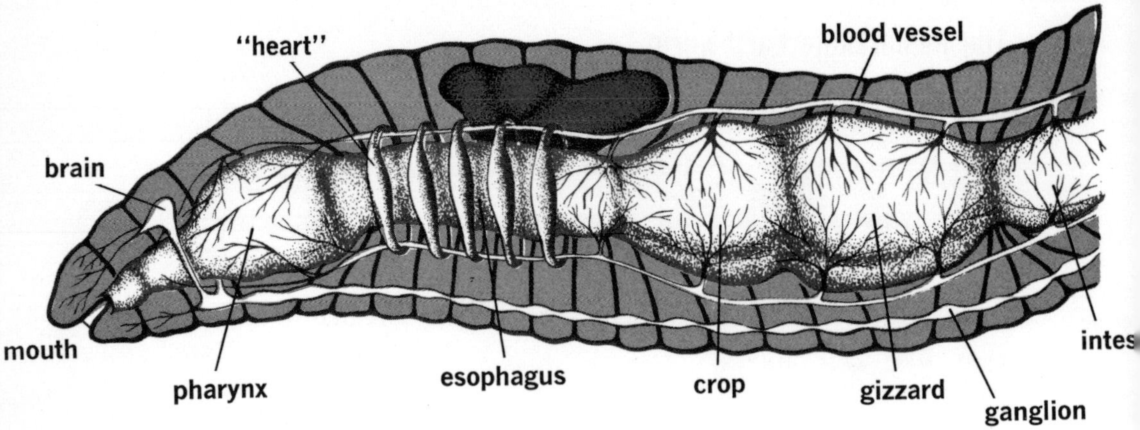


Like more complex animals (including man) the earthworm has a digestive system, a circulatory system, and a nervous system.

are sucked in, a certain amount of the soil itself is sucked in.

The food then passes down the long esophagus into the CROP. Here the earthworm can store the food for digestion later on.

From the crop the food passes into a thick pouch called the GIZZARD, where it is ground up between grains of sand. The softened, ground-up food then passes into the INTESTINE, where it is digested. Special cells in the intestine produce digestive juices that break the food down into proteins, amino acids, carbohydrates, and fats. Undigested substances, mostly soil that was sucked in with the food particles, pass out of the earthworm through an opening called the ANUS, in the last segment of the body.

Once the food is digested in the intestine of the earthworm, how is it carried to all the cells of the earthworm's body? For that matter, when you eat your food, how are the digested food substances carried to all the cells of your body?

The answer is very much the same for the earthworm and for you. The earthworm is the least complex of all animals to have a special system for transporting digested food. This is called the CIRCULATORY system. Digested food substances are carried through the circulatory system in the blood.

Around the esophagus of the earthworm there are five pairs of large blood vessels. They are sometimes called the earthworm's hearts. They are very much simpler than the human heart, but their purpose is the same—to circulate blood through the blood vessels. What happens, briefly, is that tiny blood vessels, called CAPILLARIES, absorb the food substances in the intestines. The blood passes into larger blood vessels, and is circulated around the earthworm's body by the pumping action of the five pairs of "hearts."

## How the Earthworm Breathes

The earthworm does not breathe in the same way

that you do. But each cell in its body must receive oxygen, just as each cell in your body must receive oxygen if it is to stay alive and do its special work. We have large organs to obtain oxygen—our lungs. But in the earthworm, oxygen from the air enters directly through its skin and passes into the blood through tiny capillaries.

The oxygen is not simply dissolved in the blood. It combines with a remarkable protein called hemoglobin, which can carry large quantities of oxygen. The hemoglobin is contained in special cells called red blood cells; and it is these that give blood its red color both in human beings and the earthworm.

It is not enough, though, for the body cells to receive oxygen. They must also give off carbon dioxide. This, too, is collected by the hemoglobin in the earthworm's blood, and is then released through the skin. Carbon dioxide collects in a similar way in the hemoglobin of our blood, but we release it through our lungs when we breathe out.

The earthworm's skin is thin and delicate. On the outside it is protected by a layer of cuticle. But in order for oxygen to enter and for carbon dioxide to get out, the skin and the cuticle must be moist. Therefore, special cells in the skin produce a substance called mucus; and it is this that makes an earthworm feel rather slimy when you touch it. If the earthworm's skin becomes dry it cannot live.

## Can the Earthworm Learn?

The earthworm has a nervous system that enables it to do many more things than an amoeba or a paramecium. Although it has no eyes it has groups of cells at both ends of its long body which respond to light. Shine a flashlight on an earthworm at night, and it will disappear into the ground instantly. It is also sensitive to touch, to temperature, and to vibrations such as footsteps. The famous scientist Charles Darwin was fascinated by earthworms and spent much time studying them. He found that they were sensitive to different foods: if they were given a choice they selected onion, celery, and carrot rather than cabbage. Many human beings would, too.

In the third segment from the front the earthworm has a very tiny brain. From this, two cords of nerves extend downward, forming a sort of collar around the pharynx. A long white nerve extends from the collar underneath the digestive tract all the way along the earthworm's body. A little swelling called a GANGLION appears on the nerve cord in each segment; and from each ganglion emerge the nerves controlling the activities of that segment.

This is somewhat like the nervous system of your body. From your brain a nerve cord extends downward, controlling many of your activities. But instead of being in front of your digestive tract, it runs down the back, and it is enclosed and protected by the strong vertebrae of your backbone. This is true of all animals with backbones, including fish, snakes, birds, dogs, and cats.

But animals without backbones, such as lobsters and crabs and all insects, have the same kind of nervous system as the earthworm, with the main nerve cord below the digestive tract.

Since an earthworm has a brain, does it have the ability to learn, like more complex animals? Scientists have carried out some interesting experiments to test the earthworm's learning ability. In one experiment a box was constructed in the shape of a letter T. The earthworm entered at the bottom. When it reached the crossbar of the T, the earthworm could turn to the right, where it would enter a dark moist chamber. Or it could turn to the left, where it would touch some wires and receive a slight electric shock.

The scientists found that in nine-tenths of the tests, after about two hundred trials, an earthworm would turn to the right. So, it seemed that earthworms could learn to avoid an uncomfortable situation.

But then a most interesting fact was discovered. If the earthworm lost the first five segments of its body, including its tiny brain, it still continued to turn to the right, to the warm moist chamber. Scientists are not yet sure why this happens.

Fortunately, earthworms can regenerate their first five segments—that is, they can grow a new head. So these experiments did the earthworms no serious harm.

## How the Earthworm Reproduces

In one way the earthworm is quite different from the more complex animals. Like the hydra, it is both male and female. Each earthworm produces both sperm cells and egg cells. For this reason earthworms are said to be HERMAPHRODITIC. In Greek mythology, Hermaphroditus was the son of the god

Hermes and the goddess Aphrodite; and in the myth that was told about him, his body was combined with the body of a beautiful nymph whom he loved.

The egg cells of the earthworm are produced in two ovaries, which are in segment 13, counting from the front.

The sperm cells are produced in testes, which are in segments 10 and 11.

But the sperms of an earthworm do not fertilize the egg cells of the same earthworm. What happens is that during the breeding season the earthworms come together in pairs, and they exchange their sperms.

Between segments 32 and 37, the earthworm's body appears to be thickened and swollen. This is part of the animal's reproductive system. It is called the CLITELLUM, from a Latin word meaning "pack saddle."

When two earthworms are going to exchange sperms, they come together so that their heads point in opposite directions. The clitellum of each produces mucus, which hardens into two bands, binding the earthworms close to each other.

Then the exchange of sperms takes place. Each earthworm stores away the new sperms it has received from the other, and the two earthworms separate.

Later, when one of the earthworms is ready to lay its eggs, the clitellum produces a fluid which hardens and forms a sort of girdle around its body.

Then this girdle is worked forward until it reaches segment 13. Here some eggs are passed to it from the earthworm's ovaries.

The girdle works along a little farther. Then sperms are squeezed out over the eggs, from the store of sperms which came from the other earthworm.

In this way, the egg cells are fertilized by sperms from another earthworm. This is known as CROSS-FERTILIZATION.

Finally, the girdle slips right over the earthworm's head, and closes completely around the fertilized eggs, forming a small cocoon. This lies in the soil for several weeks, until the eggs hatch and the baby earthworms come out into the world, ready to grow and live their own lives.

# A Look at Ourselves

Now we are going to take a tremendous leap forward in the story of biology. We shall not discuss in detail the animals that wear their skeletons on the outside of their bodies, such as lobsters, spiders and insects, of which there are more than 720,000 different species. Of the 45,000 different species of animals with backbones, we shall discuss only one: man. In this chapter we are going to look at ourselves.

## A Look at Ourselves

Like other multi-celled animals, man's body is made up of a multitude of cells—in this case, as we have seen, at least 10 trillion cells. The cells of the human body are organized in definite layers called TISSUES. The tissues, in turn, are organized to form ORGANS, such as the stomach—which is composed of muscle tissue, lining tissue, blood vessels, and so on. Your stomach would be of little use by itself, however. It is part of an ORGAN SYSTEM, the digestive tract, which includes your mouth, your esophagus,

The human digestive tract.

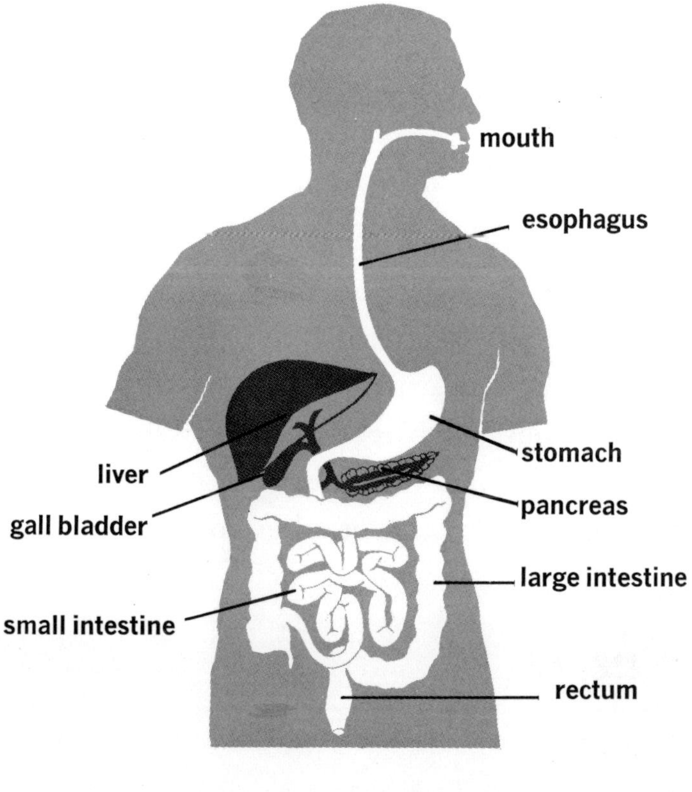

the small and large intestine, and the rectum.

But even an organ system as complicated as the digestive tract cannot work entirely alone. It depends on the system that transports blood around your body—your heart and blood vessels, and also your liver and your kidneys. It also depends on the nervous system, in which your brain is the most important organ. And it would be in a sorry state without the muscular system and the system of bones that make up your skeleton, for they help to support the various organs and carry out many important tasks.

So cells, tissues, organs, and organ systems all work together, forming a complete organism: you.

Yet this tremendously complex organism has many of the same problems as a simple little animal such as the amoeba or the paramecium or the earthworm. Each must obtain food, which must be digested and then transported through the body. (Imagine what a task it is for your body to feed those 10 trillion cells.) In addition, each form of life must obtain oxygen, and expel carbon dioxide and other wastes. We must each be able to respond to stimuli like heat or cold; otherwise we might burn or freeze to death. We must be able to move, in order to find fresh sources of food, or to escape our enemies. And to make sure that our own species continues to exist, we must reproduce.

Let us examine some of these problems in more detail and see how they are solved.

## How You Feed Your Cells

Imagine that you are sitting down to eat dinner. And let us imagine that the main course of your dinner will be roast turkey.

The taste buds on your tongue and the smell organs in your nose are affected by the sight and smell of this excellent roast turkey, and they cause certain glands in your mouth to produce a considerable amount of saliva. The saliva begins the process of digestion, and it also moistens food so that it can be swallowed more easily.

But the rest of your digestive tract is not, on the whole, greatly affected by the appetizing appearance and odor of your dinner. All that matters, once you have swallowed the roast turkey, is breaking it down into amino acids, carbohydrates, fats, and other substances you need, sending the molecules to those trillions of busy cells all over your body, and getting rid of wastes.

Roast turkey is mostly protein. Your stomach smothers it in gastric juice, which contains hydrochloric acid and a powerful enzyme called pepsin, and churns the mixture around until it is a soft, soupy mixture. This passes into the small intestine, where it is attacked by three substances which complete digestion. One, called pancreatic juice, is made by a large gland called the pancreas, which lies near the stomach; a second is called bile, and comes from the gall bladder, which is attached to the liver; the third is intestinal juice, produced by the lining of the small intestine.

Now the food is reduced to molecules that the cells of the body require and can absorb. The proteins have been broken down into about twenty amino acids, the carbohydrates have been broken down into two or three simple sugars, and there are other important substances such as fats, vitamins, and salts.

But how can all these food products escape from the small intestine and travel all over your body? They *must* do so. Otherwise they will be carried on to the large intestine and then discharged with the food substances your body does not need.

The inner surface of the small intestine has mil-

Through the villi (here magnified 50 times) food molecules pass from your small intestine into blood and lymph vessels which carry them to all parts of your body.

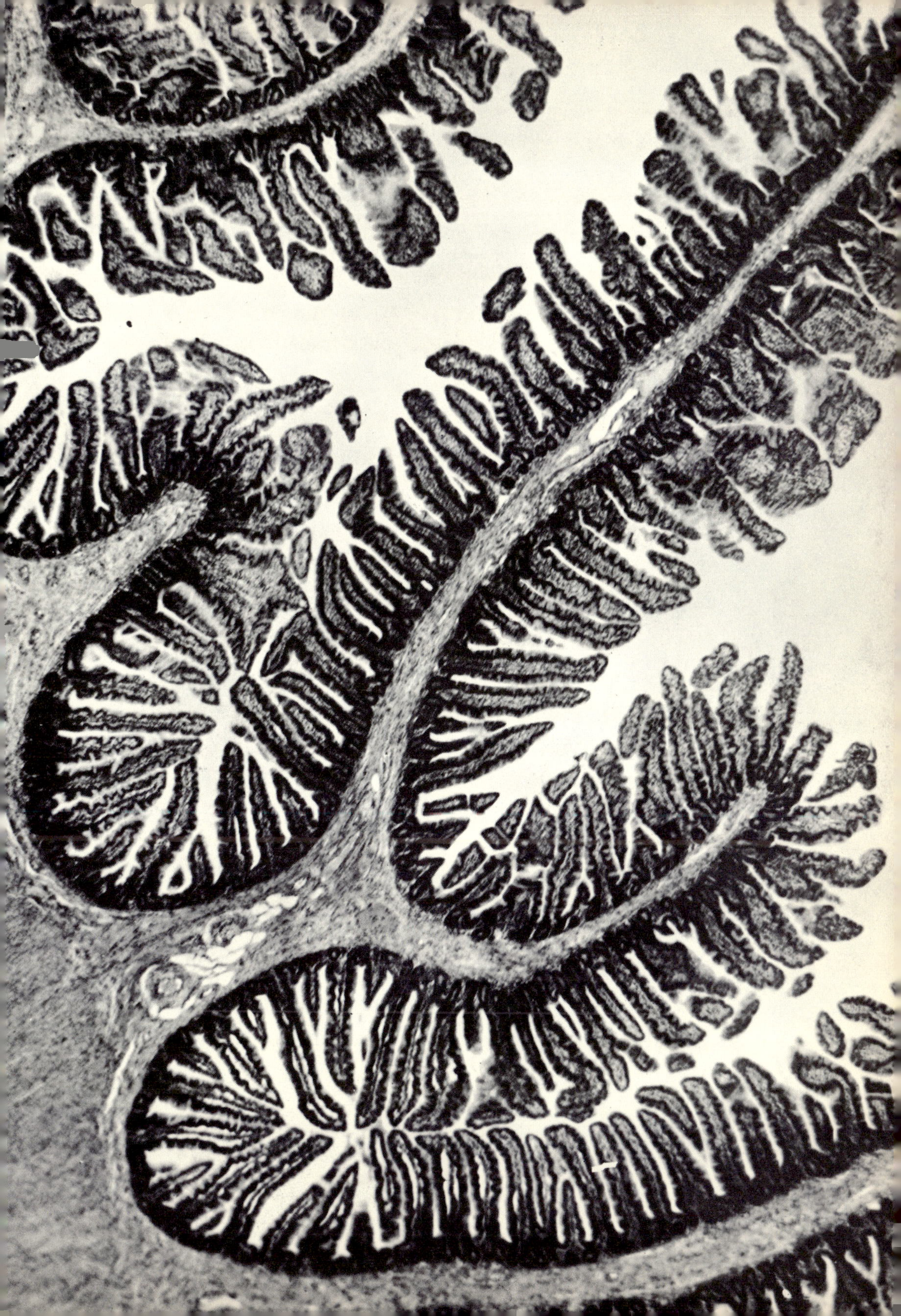

lions of very small outgrowths, like fingers, called VILLI. Each one contains tiny blood vessels, together with a tiny vessel containing a colorless fluid called LYMPH.

Fatty digested substances pass into the lymph vessels and are carried away to be stored.

The amino acids, the simple sugars, and most of the vitamins, all in the form of molecules, enter the tiny veins in the villi. Then they are carried in the blood through veins that grow larger and larger, like the branches of a tree, until they reach one of the most important organs in your body, the liver.

The liver weighs about three or four pounds in a fully grown person. It does so many things that several pages would be required to list them.

For example, it takes the simple sugars out of the blood that has come from the small intestine and changes them into another form of sugar that can be stored. It also stores the vitamin, $B_{12}$. It extracts ammonia (a poisonous substance) from the blood, and changes it into a substance called urea, which can be removed from the blood by the kidneys.

From the liver, the blood—rich in amino acids and other food molecules—travels up to the heart. Now another stage of transportation begins.

# The Work of Your Heart

The blood, so far, has been moving *toward* the heart. Blood vessels carrying blood to the heart are called VEINS. The blood in veins is called VENOUS BLOOD.

In addition to carrying food molecules, the venous blood is carrying wastes such as urea. It is also carrying carbon dioxide which has been collected from the cells. The substance that collects carbon dioxide is the wonderful hemoglobin, which you read about in the last chapter. Hemoglobin, in the red blood cells, carries oxygen or carbon dioxide with equal ease.

The heart is about the size of a large fist. It is built of very strong muscle. You can think of it, quite simply, as two pumps joined together and working side by side. Each pump has a special task.

The venous blood from all over the body enters the right side of the heart.

The heart pumps this blood to the lungs.

The lungs are filled with air you have breathed in, rich with oxygen.

The venous blood passes through a network of blood vessels in the lungs, and the hemoglobin performs another of its astonishing tricks: it exchanges

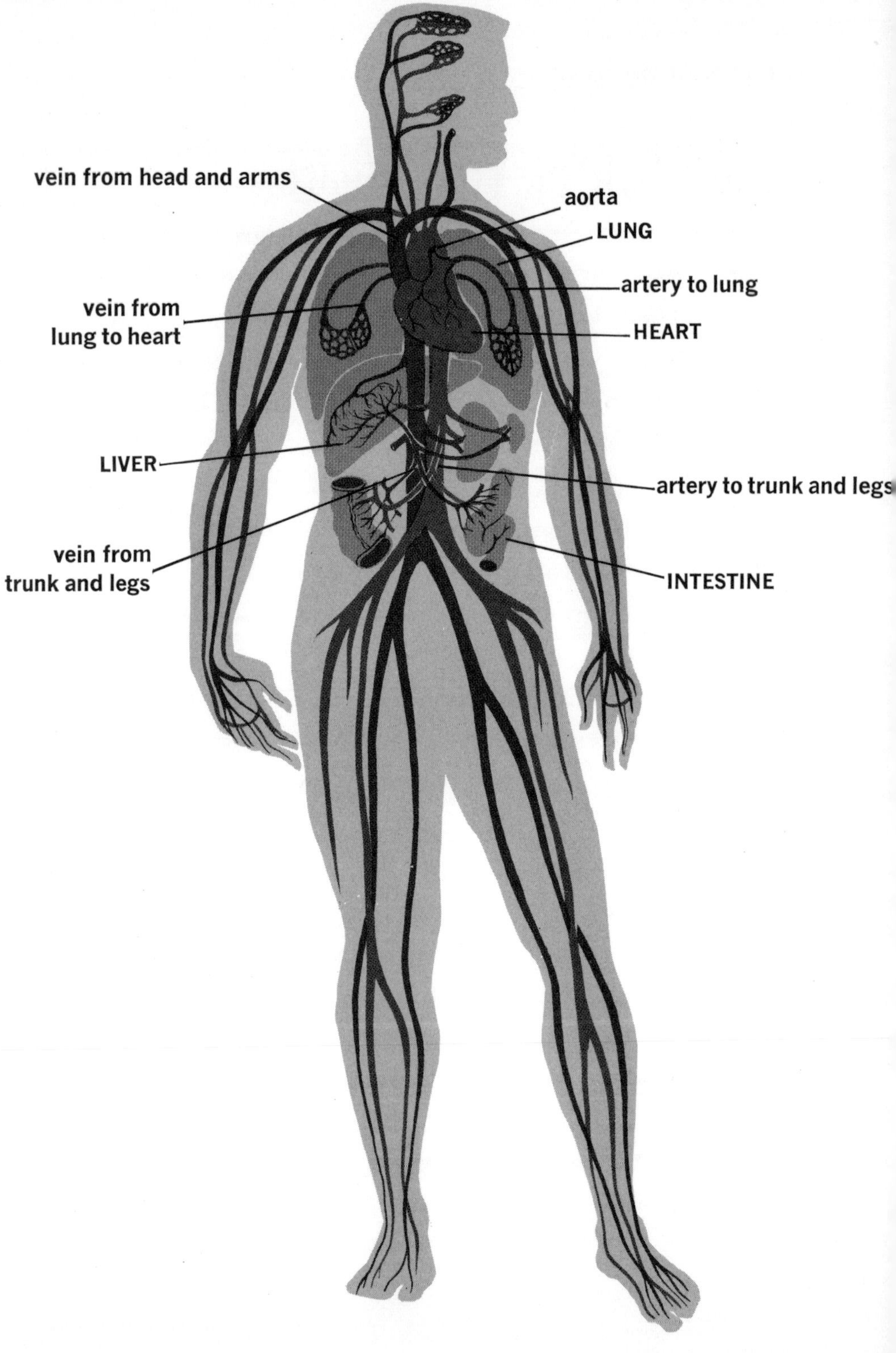

vein from head and arms
aorta
LUNG
artery to lung
vein from
lung to heart
HEART
LIVER
artery to trunk and legs
vein from
trunk and legs
INTESTINE

the carbon dioxide (which you don't need) for the oxygen (which you do need). You breathe out the air containing carbon dioxide; and the blood, now loaded with oxygen as well as food substances, returns to the left side of the heart. Now it is called ARTERIAL BLOOD, and it is a brighter red than it was before it acquired oxygen.

The left side of the heart pumps the arterial blood into a thick strong blood vessel called the AORTA. Blood vessels carrying blood away from the heart are ARTERIES. From the aorta the arterial blood passes through arteries that get smaller and smaller, like the branches of a tree, until the tiniest of all blood vessels are reached: the CAPILLARIES. From the capillaries, molecules of oxygen and food substances can move out and reach the cells. At the same time, carbon dioxide and other waste substances can enter the blood, to be carried back in the veins.

The heart is a marvelously strong organ. In your lifetime it will beat more than three billion times, pumping your blood around your body.

Part of the human circulatory system. The human body contains 60,000 to 100,000 miles of blood vessels.

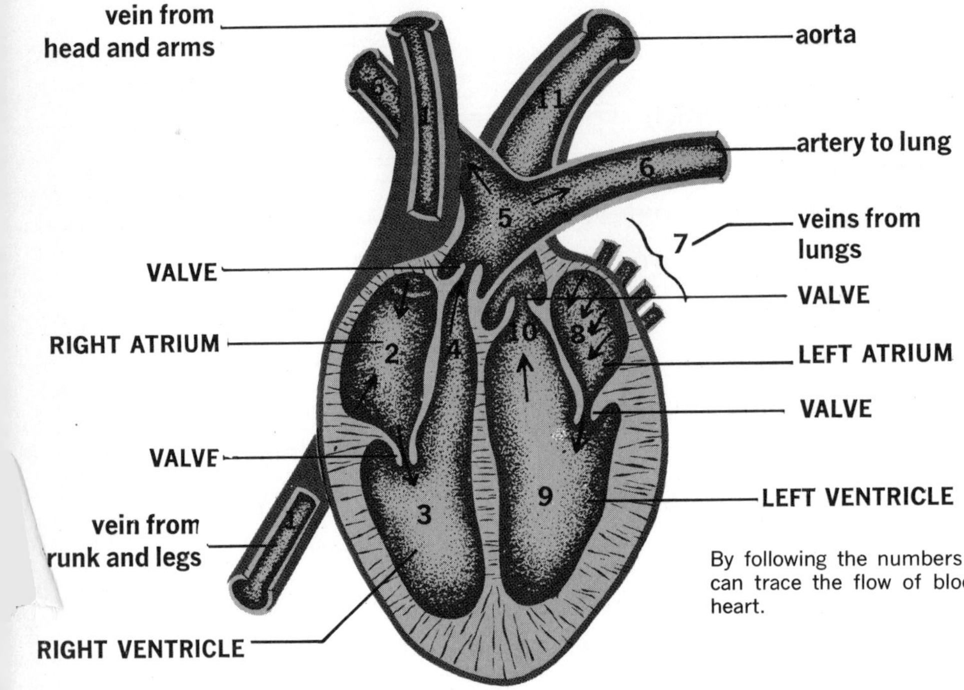


By following the numbers and arrows, you can trace the flow of blood in the human heart.

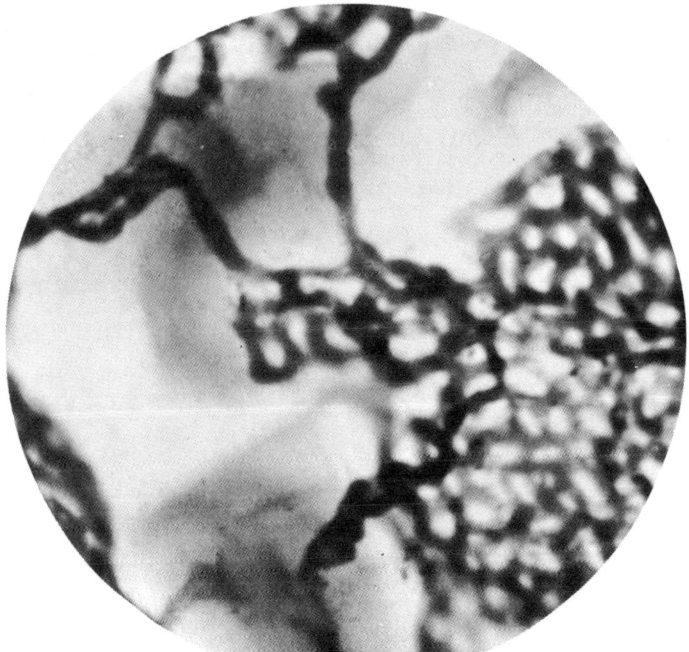

To these capillaries of the lungs (magnified 250 times), your blood brings carbon dioxide to be breathed out. Here your blood also picks up the oxygen needed throughout your body.

## How You Move and Feel and Think

The earthworm, as we have seen, moves by compressing its circular muscles, making itself thin and long, and then compressing its long muscles, making itself thick and short. It also uses its setae as levers.

You move in a different manner, using your bones as levers. The bones of your legs are the principal levers you use when you walk or run. The bones of your arms are the principal levers you use when you reach out to pick up something.

Bones can't move by themselves. They are moved by muscles. A muscle is attached to a bone in a special way, so that the bone is pulled in a certain direction when the muscle contracts.

This is not enough: the bone would be useless if it worked in one direction only, as you can observe if you raise your forearm. There must be another muscle to pull the bone in the opposite direction. The muscles that move your bones work in pairs.

But muscles can't contract by themselves. Imagine that you are swimming in a race: your arms and your legs are performing many complicated actions as they carry you through the water. How do the muscles work exactly in the right order?

The answer is: muscles are controlled by nerves. The nerves carry impulses from the brain.

In some way that scientists do not yet fully understand, the brain decides the order in which your muscles must move. The brain transmits messages that are partly chemical and partly electrical to the nerves controlling the muscles. Then each muscle contracts in the order decided upon by your brain. This causes the bones of your arms and legs to move in such a way that you find yourself swimming as fast as you can—perhaps winning the race.

Scientists are agreed that there is nothing in the world more complex than the human brain. Nor is there anything as mysterious. We know many of the things that happen in the brain, but we do not know why or how they happen. We see with our eyes, we hear with our ears, we taste with our tongue. But all sensations have to be carried to the brain before they are actually experienced, and what the brain does with them we have not yet discovered.

It is man's brain that has given him his special place in creation. His brain enables him to think, and to convey his thoughts to other human beings by means of speech, or books, or in many other ways. He can build tools, and with the tools build machines to perform the most intricate tasks. Perhaps one day man will build space ships that will investigate the planets of distant stars and report whether life exists elsewhere in the universe.

## How Human Beings Reproduce

A new human being begins at the moment when a sperm unites with an egg cell, or ovum.

Sperms are produced by the male in two small organs called TESTES. The testes are contained in a pouch of skin called the SCROTUM.

The egg cells are produced by the female in two small organs called OVARIES, lying deep inside the body. Close to each ovary is a tube called an OVIDUCT. The two oviducts lead into a pear-shaped organ called the UTERUS. This is only about three inches long, and perhaps it does not seem as if it could possibly hold a baby inside it. But it can, because the walls are thick and muscular and, at the same time, very elastic. From the uterus, an opening called the VAGINA, or birth canal, leads to the outside of the body.

An egg cell is released from one of the ovaries

about once a month, and enters the open end of the oviduct nearby. Here it may be fertilized by a sperm that has been deposited in the birth canal and has swum up through the uterus into the oviduct. If this happens, it is the start of a new life.

If the egg cell is not fertilized it continues through the oviduct to the uterus, and is discharged from the body in the process called menstruation.

But the fertilized egg cell travels down to the uterus and remains there. It implants itself in the soft moist tissue of the uterus, and proceeds to develop in a remarkable way. It divides over and over again, until there are several hundred cells. Most of these cells will go on dividing to form the EMBRYO, the name given to the new organism in the first six weeks of development. Certain cells, though, form membranes that safeguard the embryo and enable it to be nourished.

The outermost membrane is called the CHORION. Tiny extensions grow from the chorion into the tissues of the uterus, forming a kind of disc called the PLACENTA.

Inside the chorion, another membrane called the AMNION surrounds the embryo. Within the amnion is a fluid that supports the embryo and helps to protect it from injury. This fluid does not contain nourishment of any kind; it is simply a watery medium in which the embryo can develop, and which acts as an excellent shock absorber.

How does the embryo, within these membranes and surrounded by fluid, receive the food and oxygen that all living things must have?

Edges of the amnion come together, forming a tube called the UMBILICAL CORD. It contains blood vessels that connect the embryo to the placenta.

The placenta also contains blood vessels that come from the mother.

Food substances and oxygen move out of the mother's blood vessels in the placenta, pass into the blood vessels of the embryo, and are carried through the umbilical cord to the embryo's digestive tract.

Similarly, carbon dioxide and other wastes move out of the embryo's blood vessels in the placenta, pass into the blood vessels of the mother, and are carried away.

The embryo does not receive its blood directly from the mother: it makes its own blood. So the blood of a mother and her baby can be of different types.

Neither is there any connection between the nervous system of the embryo and the nervous system of the mother. During its development the embryo is a separate little individual, and everything it receives from the mother comes through the placenta.

At the end of six weeks the embryo has grown to a length of about two-thirds of an inch. Now it is called a FETUS, which comes from a Latin word meaning "offspring" or "young one." It already shows the beginnings of many organs, such as its eyes, ears, mouth, fingers, and toes.

At five months, it is nearly twelve inches long. And at the end of nine months, when it is ready to be born, it is about twenty inches long.

Birth starts as the strong muscle layers of the uterus contract, and squeeze the baby down toward the opening of the uterus. The muscle layers continue to contract and relax until the amnion breaks and the fluid inside is released. This is often called "the waters breaking." Now the baby can be pushed through the opening of the uterus into the birth canal; and from there it is only a short distance to the outside world.

The umbilical cord, which still connects the baby to the placenta, is cut and tied by the doctor. The small piece remaining on the baby will shrivel up

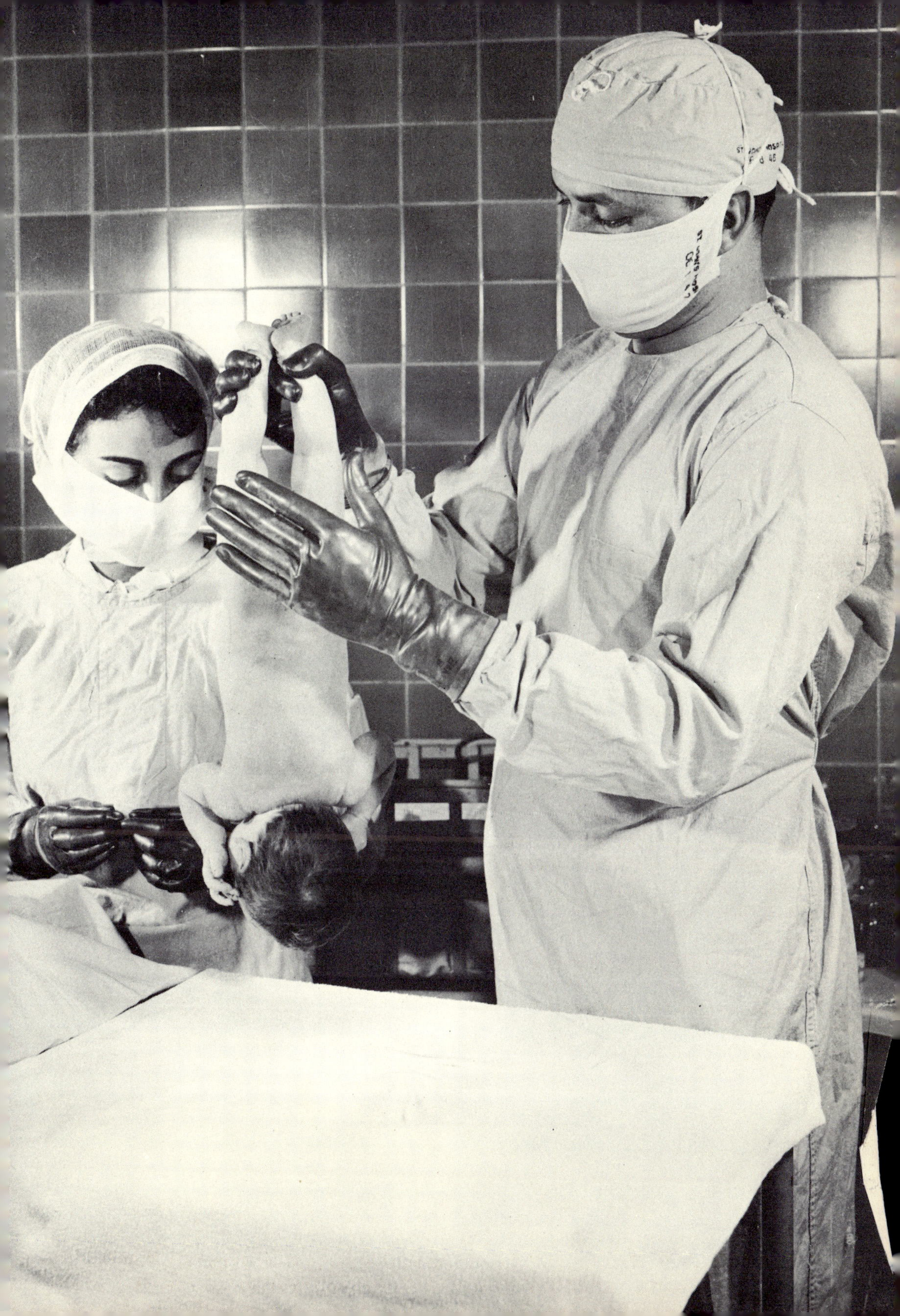

eventually, leaving only a sort of little button of skin, the navel, to mark where the umbilical cord entered the baby's body. The placenta, together with the amnion and chorion, will soon be pushed out by the contraction of the uterus. They are called the AFTERBIRTH. They have completed their vital work, and they are now of no further use.

But, until it was born, the baby was living in the fluid within the amnion. It was receiving oxygen and getting rid of carbon dioxide through the placenta, and its lungs were not working.

Usually, as soon as it is born, a baby will begin to cry lustily. This is not because it is in any pain. It is, in a way, the last stage in the process of birth. As a result of crying, its lungs fill with air; it continues to breathe; and the wonderful process of life goes on.

# Index

## Index

## About the author

Bernard Glemser is the author of *All About the Human Body,* which *Library Journal* called "one of the best physiology books for grades 5–9 yet to appear." Born in England and now a resident of New York City, Mr. Glemser has written several other books for young people and for adults.

## About the artist

Eva Cellini has been a book illustrator for many years, both in her native Hungary and, since 1956, in New York City. With her husband Joseph, she has illustrated many science books, including *The Science of Biology* by Paul B. Weisz.

## SPACE SCIENCE

**All About Satellites and Space Ships**
*by David Dietz*

**All About Rockets and Space Flight**
*by Harold D. Goodwin*

**All About the Planets**
*by Patricia Lauber*

**All About the Stars**
*by Anne Terry White*

## PHYSICAL SCIENCE

**All About the Atom**
*by Ira M. Freeman*

**All About Electricity**
*by Ira M. Freeman*

**All About Radio and Television**
*by Jack Gould*

**All About Engines and Power**
*by Sam and Beryl Epstein*

**All About the Wonders of Chemistry**
*by Ira M. Freeman*

**All About Sound and Ultrasonics**
*by Ira M. Freeman*

## NATURAL SCIENCE

**All About Animals and Their Young**
*by Robert M. McClung*

**All About Horses**
*by Marguerite Henry*

**All About Dogs**
*by Carl Burger*

**All About Monkeys**
*by Robert S. Lemmon*

**All About Whales**
*by Roy Chapman Andrews*

**All About Fish**
*by Carl Burger*

**All About Birds**
*by Robert S. Lemmon*

**All About the Insect World**
*by Ferdinand C. Lane*

**All About Moths and Butterflies**
*by Robert S. Lemmon*

**All About Snakes**
*by Bessie M. Hecht*

**All About Dinosaurs**
*by Roy Chapman Andrews*

**All About Strange Beasts of the Past**
*by Roy Chapman Andrews*

**All About Strange Beasts of the Present**
*by Robert S. Lemmon*

**All About the Flowering World**
*by Ferdinand C. Lane*

## EARTH SCIENCE

**All About the Planet Earth**
*by Patricia Lauber*

**All About Mountains and Mountaineering**
*by Anne Terry White*

**All About Volcanoes and Earthquakes**
*by Frederick H. Pough*

**All About Rocks and Minerals**
*by Anne Terry White*

**All About the Ice Age**
*by Patricia Lauber*

**All About the Weather**
*by Ivan Ray Tannehill*

**All About the Sea**
*by Ferdinand C. Lane*

**All About Sailing the Seven Seas**
*by Ruth Brindze*

**All About Undersea Exploration**
*by Ruth Brindze*

**All About Great Rivers of the World**
*by Anne Terry White*

**All About the Jungle**
*by Armstrong Sperry*

**All About the Desert**
*by Sam and Beryl Epstein*

**All About the Arctic and Antarctic**
*by Armstrong Sperry*

## PHYSIOLOGY AND MEDICINE

**All About the Human Body**
*by Bernard Glemser*

**All About Great Medical Discoveries**
*by David Dietz*

## GREAT DISCOVERIES

**All About Archaeology**
*by Anne Terry White*

**All About Prehistoric Cave Men**
*by Sam and Beryl Epstein*

**All About Famous Scientific Expeditions**
*by Raymond P. Holden*

**All About Famous Inventors and Their Inventions**
*by Fletcher Pratt*

## THE UNITED STATES

**All About Our 50 States**
*by Margaret Ronan*

**All About the U.S. Navy**
*by Edmund L. Castillo*

## MUSIC

**All About the Symphony Orchestra**
*by Dorothy Berliner Commins*

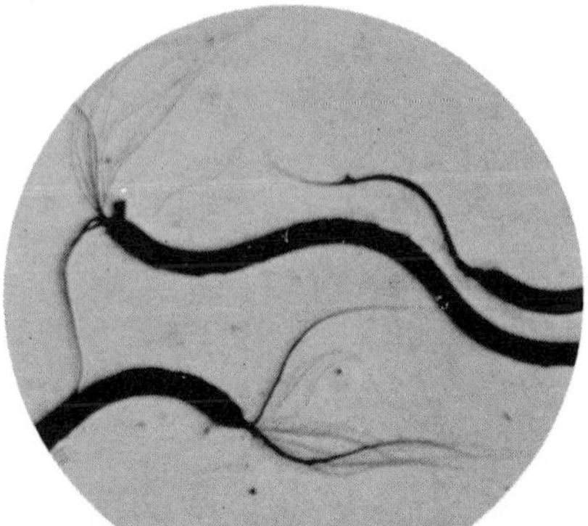
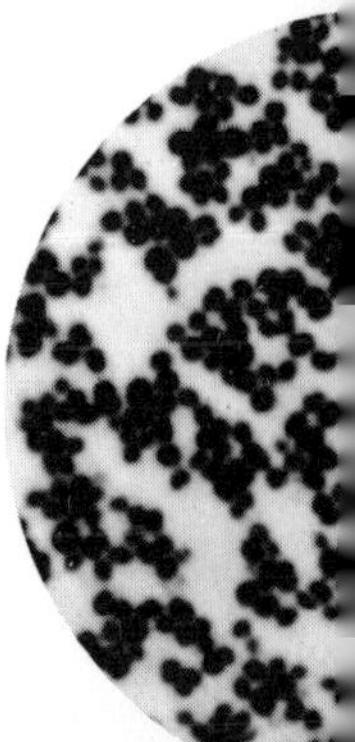

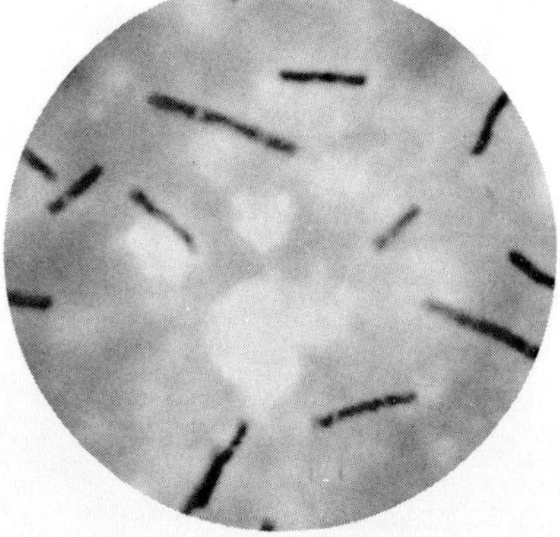

[redacted]

574 [redacted] 8.1